The
Jack Russell Terrier

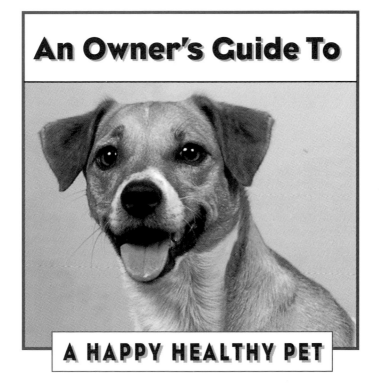

An Owner's Guide To

A HAPPY HEALTHY PET

Howell Book House

Howell Book House
A Simon & Schuster Macmillan Company
1633 Broadway
New York, NY 10019

Library of Congress Cataloging-in-Publication Data
Brown, Catherine Romaine.
    The Jack Russell terrier : an owner's guide to a happy, healthy pet / Catherine Romaine Brown.
        p. cm.
    ISBN 0-87605-483-1
    1. Jack Russell terrier.   I. Title.·
    SF429.J27B76   1996
    636.7'55—dc20   96-10847
                                    CIP

Manufactured in the United States of America
10 9 8 7 6 5 4 3

Series Director: Dominique De Vito
Series Assistant Director: Ariel Cannon
Book Design: Michele Laseau/George McKeon
Cover Design: Iris Jeromnimon
Illustration: Jeff Yesh
Photography:
Cover Photos by Paulette Braun/Pets by Paulette
Joan Balzarini: 96
Mary Bloom: 24, 96, 136, 145
Paulette Braun/Pets by Paulette: 62, 66
Bill Breakstone: 9, 17
Catherine Brown: 6, 27, 31, 36, 53, 64
Buckinghamhill American Cocker Spaniels: 148
Sian Cox: 134
Dr. Ian Dunbar: 98, 101, 103, 111, 116–17, 122, 123, 127
Sandra Feber: 68
Barry Loar: 93
Dan Lyons: 96
Laurie Mercer: 20, 21, 35, 42, 50, 60, 63, 65, 71
Cathy Merrithew: 129
Geraldine Morin: 43, 54
Liz Palika: 133
Janice Raines: 132
Susan Rezy: 44, 56
Judith Strom: 96, 107, 110, 128, 130, 135, 137, 139, 140, 144, 149, 150
Toni Tucker: 5
Michele Ward: 2–3, 10, 13, 18, 23, 28, 32, 40–41, 45, 48, 67
Kerrin Winter & Dale Churchill: 96–97

Contents

Welcome

to the

World

of the

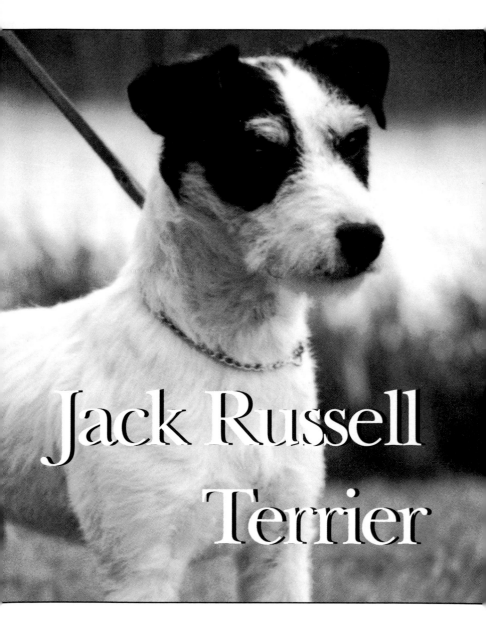

part one

Jack Russell Terrier

External Features of the Jack Russell Terrier

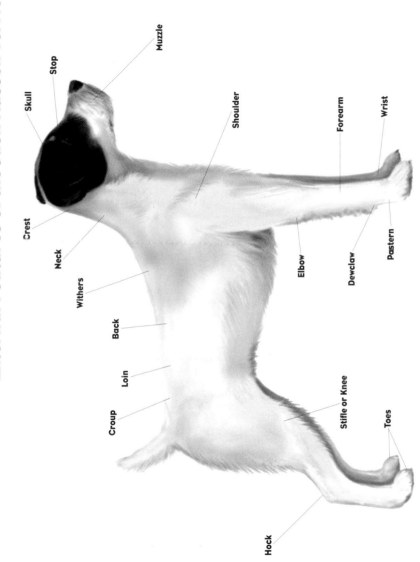

Skull

Stop

Muzzle

Crest

Neck

Shoulder

Withers

Forearm

Wrist

Elbow

Dewclaw

Pastern

Back

Loin

Croup

Stifle or Knee

Toes

Hock

chapter 1

What
Is a
Jack Russell
Terrier?

The Jack Russell Terrier, also known as the Parson Jack Russell Terrier, is small in size and big in attitude. This dog is highly intelligent and expressive, brave to the point of abandon and considered by some to be compulsive in behavior. They are also loving dogs with a great sense of humor who treasure their contact with humans. Although adaptable, this breed demands an enormous amount of physical and mental activity.

First and foremost, however, the Jack Russell is a hunting dog that works below ground. This terrier's structure is modeled after that of the vixen fox. Like the fox, the Jack Russell must be well angulated and possess a small, compressible chest that enables it to maneuver in small earthen tubes, often deeply below ground. Interestingly, the Jack Russell is not considered to be a "pure" breed but is, rather, a strain or type of Fox Terrier. The Jack Russell Terrier has a broad standard and a broad genetic makeup, and they do not necessarily breed true to type. This is the result of having been bred strictly for hunting since their beginnings in the early nineteenth century.

The Jack Russell Terrier Standard

The Jack Russell Terrier Club of America, the oldest and largest JRT breed club and registry in the world, has adopted the standard set by the JRTC of Great Britain, guidelines designed to preserve and protect this working strain of terrier. The standard appears in italics followed by the comments of this author.

The Jack Russell is an extremely energetic and lively dog.

Characteristics *The terrier must present a lively, active and alert appearance. It should impress with its fearless and happy disposition. It should be remembered that the Jack Russell is a working terrier and should retain these instincts. Nervousness, cowardice and over-aggressiveness should be discouraged, and it should always appear confident.*

The Jack Russell Terrier must be a lively, ready-for-action terrier, on its toes every waking moment. It is a dog that radiates an impressive level of fearlessness. This dog has a happy, cheerful disposition and a smile on its face, so to speak. They are trigger-quick for action, and yet not nervous or yappy. They should not be cowardly, or demonstrate fearfulness by skulking or acting timid; the JR is a hunting dog, and has been bred for courage.

The Jack Russell should not be aggressive in its relations with humans. It has been bred as a hunting dog to hold its ground with quarry, but not to do battle with the beast. The dog is meant to work with its handler, and in this capacity should appear cheerful and willing. It must never be made to feel humiliated or encouraged to be overly aggressive.

The Jack Russell's head should be in harmony with the body.

General Appearance *A sturdy, tough terrier, very much on its toes at all times, measuring between 10" and 15" at the withers. The body length must be in proportion to the height, and it should present a compact, balanced image, always being in solid, hard condition.*

The five-inch variation between minimum and maximum heights may seem unusual, but the dogs produced under this broad standard provide their owners with the variety required to meet their needs. Different types of quarry require different-sized dogs.

Head *Should be well balanced and in proportion to the body. The skull should be flat, of moderate width at the ears, narrowing to the eyes. There should be a defined stop, but not overpronounced. The length of the muzzle from the nose to the stop should be slightly shorter than the distance from the stop to the occiput. The nose should be black. The jaw should be powerful and well-boned with strongly muscled cheeks.*

The most important thing about the JR's head is that it carries the brain. The courage and intelligence necessary to survive service in the field are contained in the head.

Unlike the Fox Terrier's head, the Jack Russell's head should have a defined yet not too severe stop. The head should be in harmony with the body. A tiny, weak-looking head is not appropriate for a hunting dog, nor is a massive head that looks as though it could stop up an earth (earthen tunnel) or make the dog appear head-heavy.

WHAT IS A BREED STANDARD?

A breed standard—a detailed description of an individual breed—is meant to portray the *ideal* specimen of that breed. This includes ideal structure, temperament, gait, type—all aspects of the dog. Because the standard describes an ideal specimen, it isn't based on any particular dog. It is a concept against which judges compare actual dogs and breeders strive to produce dogs. At a dog show, the dog that wins is the one that comes closest, in the judge's opinion, to the standard for its breed. Breed standards are written by the breed parent clubs, the national organizations formed to oversee the well-being of the breed.

Eyes *Should be almond-shaped, dark in color and full of life and intelligence.*

Unlike some other breeds, the Jack Russell Terrier likes to make and hold eye contact with people. In this gesture and in the alert, intelligent look in his eyes lie the expression of the true Jack Russell character: bold, fearless and eager.

Ears *Small V-shaped drop ears carried forward close to the head and of moderate thickness.*

The ears should not stand up (prick eared). Prick ears are a sign of past infusions of other breeds or are due to thick cartilage. Thick, houndish ears are likewise not desirable. Ears that have bits missing are acceptable when exhibiting the working terrier.

Because the JRT was bred to work in the field, not in the show ring, scarred ears from encounters in the line of duty are not a defect. The terrier's ears fold over to help him in his job and are meant to protect the inner ear from dirt and other matter in the field.

Mouth *Strong teeth with the top slightly overlapping the lower. Note: A level bite is acceptable for registration.*

The standard calls for a scissors bite, though it states clearly that a level bite is also acceptable.

Neck *Clean and muscular, of good length, gradually widening at the shoulders.*

Forequarters *Shoulders should be sloping and well laid back, fine at points and clearly cut at the withers. Forelegs should be strong and straight-boned with joints in correct alignment. Elbows hanging perpendicular to the body and working free of the sides.*

The laid-back angle of the shoulder blade specified in this part of the standard allows good movement at the front end of the dog.

Body *The chest should be shallow, narrow and the front legs set not too widely apart, giving an athletic rather than a heavily chested appearance. As a guide only, the chest should be small enough to be easily spanned behind the shoulders, by average-sized hands, when the terrier is in fit, working condition. The back should be strong, straight and, in comparison to the height of the terrier, give a balanced image. The loin should be slightly arched.*

The chest size and shape are of utmost importance. A barrel- or keel-shaped chest would hinder the dog's ability to make its way through narrow passages below ground. A small, flexible chest that can be compressed in a tight place is vital, as a chesty dog cannot get far into an earthen tube.

The chest of the Jack Russell must be the correct size and shape for the dog to do the job it was bred for.

Hindquarters *Should be strong and muscular, well put together with good angulation and bend of stifle, giving plenty of drive and propulsion. Looking from behind, the hocks must be straight.*

Feet *Round, hard-padded and of catlike appearance, turning neither in nor out.*

Good, compact, well-padded feet are very important to this working dog, as Jack Russells must be able to dig efficiently in various soil conditions.

Tail *Set rather high, carried gaily and in proportion to body length, usually about four inches long, providing a good hand-hold.*

The approximately four-inch docked tail provides a good hand-hold for extracting the terrier from an earth tunnel when necessary. Undocked tails carry the risk of breaking while the dog backs up in tiny tunnels, and tails that are too short don't provide a good terrier-handle. A scant one-third of a puppy's tail is docked when it is around three days old. Dewclaws are also removed so they don't catch and tear while the dog is working.

White should be the dominant color in the Jack Russell's coat.

Coat *Smooth, without being so sparse as not to provide a certain amount of protection from the elements and undergrowth. Rough- or broken-coated, without being woolly.*

Since JRTs must spend hours below ground in dark, damp places, a good coat is necessary to provide protection. When traveling on the ground, a good coat protects the skin from thorns and helps to resist burdocks.

Color *White should predominate (i.e., more than 51 percent white) with tan, black or brown markings. Brindle markings are unacceptable.*

White has been favored partly because it was thought that hounds would be better able to distinguish the terrier from the fox, and partly so that a handler, after digging to the dog, would be able to immediately distinguish the quarry from the dog when both were covered with loose soil.

Gait   *Movement should be free, lively, well coordinated, with straight action in front and behind.*

All that is favored in the good movement of a correct and beautiful horse applies to the movement of the terrier.

Please note: For showing purposes, terriers are classified into two groups: 10" to 12½" and over 12½" up to 15".

Here is where there is room for variety for different purposes. It is perhaps like a good selection of tools for a job that allows for scope and variety in the job. Sometimes the working terrier person desires tweezers for a job, sometimes a wrench. Different types of quarry may require different sizes and working styles.

Old scars or injuries, the result of work or accident, should not be allowed to prejudice a terrier's chance in the show ring unless they interfere with its movement or utility for work or stud.

Some working terriers may lose teeth while working from biting and pulling through roots in their paths, and some are injured in encounters with an earth-dwelling resident. As long as the jaw is in correct alignment and its movement is not affected, such injuries are not counted against the terrier in the show ring.

Male animals should have two apparently normal testicles fully descended into the scrotum.

A Jack Russell Terrier should not show any strong characteristics of another breed.

Since the Jack Russell is a strain of Fox Terrier, influences from other breeds may sometimes surface in markings (such as brindle) or in soft or linty coat textures.

Faults   *Shyness. Disinterest. Overly aggressive. Defects in bite. Weak jaws. Fleshy ears. Down at shoulder. Barrel ribs. Out at the elbow. Narrow hips. Straight stifles. Weak feet. Sluggish or unsound movement. Dishing. Plaiting. Toeing. Silky or woolly coats. Too much color (less than 51 percent* *white). Shrill or weak voice. Lack of muscle or skin tone. Lack of stamina or lung reserve. Evidence of foreign blood.*

The "Faults" section of the standard directly reflects the work the JRT was bred to do. A dog lacking the necessary characteristics is not a good example of the working JRT, though he may still be a wonderful pet.

The dog must be able to move well because its success below ground depends on its being able to do so. Defects of structure may hinder a dog and cause its demise if it is unable to work free from a small earthen tube. The terrier must speak below ground to mark the location of its quarry, so a good voice is desirable. In the early days of terrier work, the handler depended on the voice of his dog in order to locate the dog while digging. Now there are bleeper devices, with transmitters and locaters, but the good voice of the dog remains important. A working terrier must be in prime condition, not unfit with soft muscles or loose skin. The terrier must be an athlete, up to the work required. In the past, there were infusions of other breeds such as the Lakeland, Border and Black & Tan Terriers, among others, but the Jack Russell should no longer show any strong evidence of these old crosses.

The Jack Russell Terrier Club of America

The Jack Russell Terrier Club of America, The Jack Russell Terrier Club of Great Britain, and the majority of the rest of the Jack Russell clubs in the world, united through the Jack Russell Terrier World Federation, strongly oppose recognition of this breed by any kennel club or national all-breed registry. Jack Russell owners and working terrier people seem to be in complete agreement on this point and its importance in preserving the working ability, high intelligence, sound physical structure and broad standard of this terrier. A Jack Russell is not a "show dog." It is a dog with a job to do and a boundless desire to get it done.

The Jack Russell Terrier Club of America (JRTCA), founded by Ailsa Crawford in 1976, has developed one of the most unique registries in the world. It has been specifically designed to maintain the Jack Russell Terrier as a healthy working breed, as free as possible from genetic faults and characteristics that would be detrimental to the breed and its working heritage.

Unlike kennel clubs, which register entire litters at birth, the JRTCA considers an application for registration on the individual terrier's own merits—having registered parents does not automatically guarantee that the progeny can be registered.

The JRTCA does not register Jack Russells until they are a year old and conform to the high standards of health and soundness the club requires.

JRTCA STANDARDS OF EXCELLENCE

A terrier is not eligible for registration with the JRTCA until it reaches one year of age and has attained adult height, dentition and other aspects of full maturity. The owner must be a current member in good standing of the JRTCA and every application for registration must be accompanied by the following documents:

Veterinary Certificate A JRTCA Veterinary Certificate, designed specifically for the Jack Russell Terrier, must be completed and signed by a licensed veterinarian. For registration, the form must state that the dog has been examined and found to be free

13

of such inherited defects as incorrect bite, hernia, luxated patella, cryptorchidism, monorchidism, eye problems, and so on. (These are discussed at length in Chapter 7.)

Pedigree A copy of a complete pedigree, signed by the breeder, showing at least three, but preferably four, full generations. The JRTCA will not accept for registration any terrier that is determined to be inbred as defined by the club's policy, that is, no father-to-daughter, son-to-mother or brother-to-sister matings are allowed. Half-brother to half-sister is allowed only once in three generations.

Stud Service Certificate A Stud Certificate is completed and signed by the owner of the sire, verifying that his or her dog was bred to the dam of the terrier applying for registration.

Color Photographs Photographs of the terrier standing on a firm surface, clearly showing the front and each side of the dog, are required in order to evaluate the dog's general adherence to the breed standard.

If the terrier does not meet the requirements for registration, there is a recording system available, making the recorded terrier eligible, upon qualification, for Trial and Natural Hunting Certificates.

WORKING QUALIFICATIONS

Trial Certificate Awarded by a sanctioned working judge, a Trial Certificate is for a terrier's successful work in an artificial earth at any sanctioned Jack Russell Terrier Trial.

Sporting Certificate A Sporting Certificate is awarded to those terriers who have successfully worked to nonformidable quarry such as squirrels, rats, and so on.

Natural Hunting Certificate This is awarded for natural earthwork by terrier and owner, in the field, with a JRTCA-sanctioned working judge. The dog must locate appropriate quarry, out of sight, in the ground or a rock den, and must cause the quarry to bolt from the earth or must stay with its opponent until dug to. The dog may be called out after its work but, in that case, it must be determined that the dog was right up to the quarry.

JRTCA Bronze Medallion The highest award given to a proven working terrier is the JRTCA Bronze Medallion for Special Merit in the Field, which is given to the exceptional Jack Russell who has received Natural Hunting Certificates for successfully working to three or more different quarry.

STYLE AND PURPOSE

By tradition, the terrier is bred to be "soft." The dog is not to harm the animal it meets in its lair below ground but he must have the courage to bolt it, forcing the quarry to leave its den through a tunnel and out an exit simply as a result of the brave little dog's presence. If the quarry will not or cannot bolt, the terrier should have the heart to stay with it while the owner digs down to the dog and his prize.

What, then, is the Jack Russell Terrier? It is, simply, an extension of the early unspoiled-by-show-ring-fashions strain of working Fox Terrier. It is vital to the future of this breed that potential owners know that the breed is, first and foremost, a hunting dog that has been kept sound through years of breeding strictly for working ability, temperament and intelligence. It is a little dog with a big heart who is happiest doing what it is bred to do: working hard to please its owner, and itself, in the field. Strong bonds are formed between owner and dog, to the point that they often can communicate with the mere wave of a hand or nod of a head. The observation has been made more than once that a Jack Russell can easily read a person's mind with uncanny accuracy.

Those who become charmed by the Jack Russell often lose interest in other breeds, with the possible exception of hounds or lurchers, who make good working partners for the terrier. But, placed in the wrong environment, many JRs become unruly and unwanted, requiring rescue from confused owners. Often, through education, motivated owners are able to adjust their life-styles and keep their terrier, but it cannot be stressed too strongly that the Jack Russell is not the dog for everyone.

chapter 2

The
Jack Russell
Terrier's
Ancestry

The Reverend John Russell (1795–1883) of Devonshire, in the western part of England, developed one the world's finest strains of working terriers. These terriers were bred to work. Jack Russell was a colorful and flamboyant character, and he and his strain of terriers soon became well known.

The Fox Terrier

The original strains of Fox Terriers were based on what

were called White Terriers, which now are extinct. Many British hunt kennels kept their own strains of terriers that worked with their hounds. The hounds would follow the fox in chase and put him to ground. The hounds and the field of riders following them would be moved back, and a terrier man or hunt staff member would enter a terrier after the fox. Quite often, just the presence of the baying

17

little dog would suggest to the fox that he might wish to go elsewhere for refuge—and the chase would continue.

Since the terrier ran with hounds and put in a hard day's work, good stamina and tenacity were required. The dog needed an inner flame to do such work. Often he had to know how to cut corners to catch up with the hounds, or even anticipate where the chase might end, to do his job right.

THE FOX TERRIER IN THE SHOW RING

The popularity of the terriers reached its zenith in the late nineteenth century, and Fox Terriers were accepted as an English Kennel Club breed. Popular fashion tends to require change, and it was not long before the Fox Terrier was caught up in the whims of the show ring.

*The Jack
Russell today
is similar in
form and
function to the
working Fox
Terrier of the
1800s.*

The breed developed an upright scapula (shoulder blade), a deepened chest and a lengthened, narrowed

head. In the show ring a smooth coat was favored over the less popular but more protective wiry-haired coat (rough or broken coat). The show ring's Fox Terrier was no longer at all like the working terriers in the hunt kennels. With its redesigned structure, it could not enter shallow earth even if the instinct to do so remained.

Russell himself was a member of England's Kennel Club (he was one of the original founders in 1873, and judged Fox Terriers at the first sanctioned show in 1874), but he did not exhibit his own dogs. Apparently disapproving of the changes in the terriers, he stated: "True terriers they were, but differing from the present show dogs as the wild eglantine differs from a garden rose."

The Working Terrier

As the popular Fox Terrier went to the shows, John Russell and other working terrier men went into the fields and followed hounds in pursuit of quarry. Many a man lacking wealth or a fine horse would keep a few terriers. Ordinary working men could enjoy time away from their regular chores in activity with their dogs. The ability of a good working dog to afford a man some sport locating fox or badger meant more than any pedigree. With the limited transportation available in those days, the terriers were rather closely bred. The best local working dogs were bred to local bitches, and definite types began to develop region by region, with size and temperament suitable to the area. All of these types were called "hunt" or "fox" terriers.

The Reverend Jack Russell

John Russell's dogs were of a type suitable to the terrain of the west country where they lived. But, with the fame of both Reverend Russell and his dogs spreading, it became the desirable thing in other parts of the country to have one of his terriers. Apart from his church activities, the reverend was well known throughout England as a man passionate for the sport of fox hunting and breeding fox hunting dogs. It was not long before the name Jack Russell Terrier spread and began to develop as the permanent name of these feisty little working terriers.

The reverend's foundation bitch was named Trump. In 1819, while still an undergraduate at Oxford University, he bought her from a milkman in the Oxfordshire village of Marston. In Russell's eyes, Trump was the ideal terrier. She was white with brown ears, a patch of brown over each eye and one no larger than a British penny at the base of her tail. Her coat was reported to be thick, close and wiry, but not the long jacket of the Scottish terrier. Her legs were as straight as arrows, her feet were perfect and she was of a size that has been compared to a grown vixen (female) fox. Said Russell of this lovely animal: "Her

**FAMOUS
OWNERS OF
JACK
RUSSELL
TERRIERS**

Bette Midler

Mariah Carey

Audrey
Hepburn

Andrew
Wyeth

Prince Charles

James Herriot

19

whole appearance gave indications of courage, endurance and hardihood." Even now, there is a painting of Trump hanging in the harness room of the royal residence at Sandringham, in Norfolk, England.

In England, the red fox was considered a varmint, a killer of spring lambs and poultry, so if the hunt crossed a farmer's land, risking damage to crops and fences, it was considered appropriate to kill the plentiful foxes encountered during the hunt. In America, there is little, if any, interest in harvesting foxes. Americans concentrate on the chase, and the greatest admirers of the fox are those who have spent time observing them and their intelligent strategies. Foxes in our country have many safe escape routes and seem to exhibit a sense of humor about the hounds "singing" their scent. Country sport affords a participant the pleasure of the sights and sounds of good hound work, and the enjoyment of following the hounds on horseback.

The Reverend Jack Russell was a flamboyant character who adored his hounds and hunting.

It has been reported that John Russell was also not interested in the killing of the fox. He said of the terriers: "A real Fox Terrier is not meant to murder and his intelligence should always keep him from such a crime." When fair terrier work is possible, with a noncombative terrier employed, one can well understand John Russell's fondness for the chase alone. He was a participant well into his eighties.

Russell became vicar of Swymbridge in 1832 and was occupied by both his church duties and his position as Master of Foxhounds. His circle of friends included other Masters of Foxhounds and often, even late in his life, he would travel long distances to meets. Legend has it that the bishop of his diocese once accused him of refusing to bury a body on a Wednesday because it interfered with the hunt. There are also stories of the bishop repeatedly asking Russell to give up his hounds and hunting. He agreed to give up his hounds. "Mrs. Russell shall keep them," he said.

Trump was the Reverend Jack Russell's ideal terrier.

After Jack Russell

Upon Jack Russell's death, at the age of eighty-eight, his stock was scattered. It is doubtful that anyone today can trace a terrier back to Trump.

What does live on is his strain or type of hardy, old-fashioned, willing-to-work terrier. Those who did not hunt were culled along the way, or kept as pets in homes of nonsporting people. Others that did not conform correctly for earth work, perhaps having too much blood of other breeds, were kept by people who found they were useful above ground for the task of rodent control. Some of these dogs had short bandy legs and barrel chests. They may have carried some Dachshund or Bull Terrier blood.

Many of these pet strains came to the United States with fanciers who brought them from England. With them also came fine examples of the hardy, well-conformed working terrier so favored by the Reverend Russell himself. Fortunately, while the show-ring Fox Terrier continued to develop—and change—devoted fans of the

Welcome to
the World
of the Jack
Russell Terrier

original Fox Terrier continued to happily breed and work their tough little dogs in both England and North America. During this time they were still called by many names: hunt terrier, white terrier (after their extinct ancestor) and working Fox Terrier. Eventually, of course, the problem was settled. With the name Fox Terrier being so firmly, and publicly, connected to the show dog, the name Jack Russell Terrier became attached to the original strain of working terriers.

The Jack Russell Terrier Today

The Jack Russell Terrier Club of America was founded in 1976. Twenty years later, thousands of members are united in admiration of and dedication to the protection of the Jack Russell Terrier.

Why does the Jack Russell need "protection"? Why do most of the Jack Russell Terrier clubs and the Jack Russell Terrier United World Federation oppose recognition by any all-breed kennel club? Showing dogs in highly competitive conformation contests has resulted in physical and mental changes to nearly every breed in history. While this kind of competition may be fine for other breeds, it is not suitable for the Jack Russell as it has nothing to do with the dog's ability to perform the task it was bred to do. Those loyal to the Jack Russell as it exists today will not support kennel club recognition for this extraordinary dog.

The Fox Terrier was once the dog now known as the Jack Russell. However, today's Fox Terrier no longer has the conformational structure or even the desire to perform its original function of bolting foxes from their earthen dens. The Jack Russell Terrier today is the unspoiled working terrier of the 1800s. The breed has been preserved by the working-related standards of most of the major terrier clubs. The

---

WHERE DID DOGS COME FROM?

It can be argued that dogs were right there at man's side from the beginning of time. As soon as human beings began to document their own existence, the dog was among their drawings and inscriptions. Dogs were not just friends, they served a purpose: There were dogs to hunt birds, pull sleds, herd sheep, burrow after rats—even sit in laps! What your dog was originally bred to do influences the way it behaves.

mental and physical soundness of the Jack Russell Terrier is protected by those dedicated to their breed's work, performance and character.

Fierce protection of these traits motivates loyalty to the breed, and the members of the Jack Russell Terrier Club of America are devoted to the organization and its task. Through understanding, the club can continue protecting this remarkable terrier.

Today, the Jack Russell is a much-loved pet in homes and families across the country. In addition to preserving the working function of the Jack Russell Terrier, the JRTCA serves to educate pet owners about the unique qualities and requirements of keeping a Jack Russell. The JRTCA offers services and activities to keep people working and bonding with these special dogs. The club encourages people to love, play with and work their terriers, and to fight for the dog's ability to work, both now and in the future.

Jack Russells have been preserved as working terriers from their earliest days.

THE JACK RUSSELL AS A PET

Jack Russell Terriers these days continue as adaptable and amusing companions. Still comfortable around stables, they have no fear of the large horses in their lives. They may do well with some other breeds of dogs, but not all, much preferring the company of their own. Even then, care must be exercised. They are quite sensitive and, if harshly punished, slow to forgive—if they forgive at all. Being struck is a mortal blow to the heart of this little dog and they will not tolerate abuse of any kind, especially from young children. If not totally saddened in spirit, their reaction is to retaliate in self-protection.

There are countless stories of intolerance within their own ranks, so it is well noted never to keep more than two Jack Russells together without supervision—and keeping two of the same sex together is not recommended at all. They are inclined to have serious scraps, and same-sex fighting is well known within the breed. Young puppies cannot be left with adult Russells; pups can be annoying after awhile and may end up being hurt or even killed by the adult. Being pack animals, these dogs will sometimes create a frenzy, with tragic consequences. They are cute, indeed, but have a side that must always be managed with proper guidance and control from their human "pack leaders."

The JR is irresistibly charming, but he requires great energy and attention from his owners.

Those who love this breed and understand their special needs do not recommend urban life for the modern JR. The stresses of confinement in cramped areas with limited outlets for their natural curiosity, and the sometimes compulsive behavior of an unemployed working dog, create a recipe for destruction. There are true stories of JRs in apartments who bored holes in walls or dug their way into subflooring in search of mice during times they were left alone. This is a breed that hates to be left alone and will not allow itself to be ignored. This big dog in a little body is brave to the point of abandon; few die of old age. The ones who have survived that long were fortunate enough to have been the companions of people who understood and respected their unique personality and needs.

Famous Jack Russells

Nipper, the RCA dog, is a well-recognized corporate image—one of many JRs who appear in movies as well as television ads pulling dandelions and parachuting from planes with bags of pretzels. And there is the wonderful Wishbone, the canine star of the children's show of the same name. With a human voice helping him along, he takes the part of characters in classic novels, including dressing in period costumes. In the popular sitcom *Frasier*, the Jack Russell called Eddie, whose real name is Moose, appears to be not only clever but perfectly behaved.

All of this media exposure has added to the surge in popularity of this breed in recent years. Unfortunately, it has also led all too many people to believe that all JRs are just like their movie and television counterparts.

The down side of this is that these well-intentioned people soon find themselves the frustrated owners of bundles of more energy than they can handle. With this rise in popularity has come a frightening rise in abandoned and abused Jack Russells. Moose ("Eddie") is as active and mischievous as his contemporaries, but his trainer, Matilde DeCagny, has taught him well to play his part and perform his scene-stealing antics. Wishbone and Moose are actors on television shows, and those shows do not come close to portraying all there is to know about Jack Russell Terriers, though it does show what they are capable of if provided with loving guidance, attention and a tireless teacher.

In addition to famous dogs, there are also many famous people who are serious fans of these dogs. The royal family of England has kept Jack Russells for many years, including King Edward VII, Prince Charles and Sarah Ferguson. James Herriot, the English veterinarian who authored *All Creatures Great and Small*, was presented with a JR by his wife after he told her of his admiration for the dog. Singers Bette Midler and Mariah Carey keep Jack Russells; actors Michael Douglas and Jim Carrey are fanciers, as was the late William Holden. Audrey Hepburn was deeply devoted to her little pack of JRs, and artist Jamie Wyeth included the family's Jack Russell in a portrait he painted of his wife.

chapter 3

The **World**

According to the

Jack Russell Terrier

Before you bring a Jack Russell Terrier into your home, please consider it carefully and be sure you can provide for all of the needs of this small-in-size, big-in-attitude dog. Here is a dog small enough to be spanned by average-sized hands around the largest part of his chest and, being small, he appeals to many people for all the wrong reasons. It is a mistake to

think that being small makes a Jack Russell easy to keep. Though described in one recent classified advertisement as "the designer dog of the '90s," a Jack Russell should never be chosen or thought of as a "fashion accessory." The JR is a solid bundle of energy in a deceptively small package, an intelligent, demanding, always active hunting dog.

27

There are many pleasures in owning a Jack Russell, and he can change your life, perhaps forever. If you decide that you really do want to share your life with such a bright companion, you will find that you have embarked on a wonderful adventure in friendship and admiration for one of the most remarkable, energetic canine personalities ever created.

A Working Dog

The Jack Russell, whose ancestors worked for a living hunting below ground, remains much the same animal it was nearly two hundred years ago. One of the most intelligent dogs on (or in) the earth, with an activity level locked in the "on" position, Jack Russells are indisputably active and assertive. After a nap, they are ready for seemingly endless play or work. If they cannot find a partner to play ball, they have been known to carry the ball to the top of a flight of stairs, release it, chase it down the steps and catch it before it hits bottom. A dog named Archie used to torment his family for the ball with which to play this game. No matter where in the house it was hidden, Archie would shift his JRT sense of smell into high gear, cruise the house, and find his toy. His desire to play was constant and no hiding place was sacred.

Jack Russells have been bred to dig, so it's important to be creative and thorough when considering ways to contain them.

Jack Russells Need Supervision

Jack Russells respond quickly and forcefully to their hunting instincts. The most obedient, well-trained Jack Russell, out by himself or walking unleashed at your side, is likely to bolt at the sight of a squirrel or other animal on the other side of the road. A car or truck coming along at just the wrong moment can bring a sad end to your wonderful companion. Vehicular accidents are the most common cause of death to Jack Russells—and are, for the most part, avoidable. When their instincts take over, JRs do not hesitate and are completely unaware of impending danger, so it's up to the owner keep this in mind and protect the JR from dangerous situations.

Containing a Jack Russell can be difficult. They are bred to dig and can quickly escape under a sloppily built fenced area, particularly if the fence has not been buried a few inches into the ground. These dogs can jump more than four feet from a standstill and can climb, almost human-style, over a ten-foot or higher fence. They certainly will not tolerate being tied up by a rope or chain—unthinkable for any dog, but especially for a Jack Russell. One form of confinement can be provided by invisible fencing, which uses a radio signal correction (delivered by a special collar worn by the dog) when territorial limits have been reached. The signal cannot be avoided by jumping over or digging under the line, and is respected when all else seems to fail. Unfortunately, the barrier will not keep other dogs from coming into the yard. Kennel runs are excellent if they are long enough for the dog to move about freely and provide shade and shelter. They also should have a secure top to discourage climbing.

Essentially, Jack Russells need endless protection from themselves.

A DOG'S SENSES

Sight: With their eyes located farther apart than ours, dogs can detect movement at a greater distance than we can, but they can't see as well up close. They can also see better in less light, but can't distinguish many colors.

Sound: Dogs can hear about four times better than we can, and they can hear high-pitched sounds especially well. Their ancestors, the wolves, howled to let other wolves know where they were; our dogs do the same, but they have a wider range of vocalizations, including barks, whimpers, moans and whines.

Smell: A dog's nose is his greatest sensory organ. His sense of smell is so great he can follow a trail that's weeks old, detect odors diluted to one-millionth the concentration we'd need to notice them, even sniff out a person under water!

Taste: Dogs have fewer taste buds than we do, so they're likelier to try anything—and usually do, which is why it's especially important for their owners to monitor their food intake. Dogs are omnivores, which means they eat meat as well as vegetable matter like grasses and weeds.

Touch: Dogs are social animals and love to be petted, groomed and played with.

29

They are devil-may-care, go-for-the-gusto, compulsive hunters who will seize any opportunity they can find to run toward the horizon with their noses to the ground in search of adventure.

The very same Jack Russell who lovingly curls up in your lap and shares your bed will happily dash out the door, leaving you in the lurch as he runs off to go to work below ground. How frightening it is when your JR is gone and cannot be found. It happens quite often. These dogs are primarily ruled by their instincts and their presence must never be taken for granted.

It is also unsafe to leave out the roast or a plate of butter anywhere within jumping or climbing distance. And in the time it takes you to walk to the mailbox, this little dynamo can make confetti out of the contents of a wastepaper basket.

Forget the running commentary on how you disapprove of your dog's antics; he probably isn't listening. A JR is always sure of himself and can be quite single-minded about whatever he is focused on. He can be stubborn and persist in his activity to the point of exhaustion.

Jack Russells Are Loving

Although JRs can be naughty, willful and wayward, they are quite devoted to, and want to be with, their favorite people. In fact, they can be quite possessive about those they love, wanting to guard them from children and even other pets.

Unlike many other types of dogs, Jack Russells enjoy direct eye contact. They will stare affectionately into the eyes of those they love, seemingly able to follow conversations and letting you know, in their own way, that they know what you are thinking. They are as likely (or sometimes more likely) to train their owners as their owners are to train them. They enjoy endless hours of activity and play, knowing just how to entice you into their games, and, of course, desire close physical contact with their loved ones.

They will happily cuddle up to their owners under the covers, or at least sleep near enough so they know when their people stir and are sure not to miss anything. As a whole, JRs remain almost puppylike through adulthood. They are willing, and happy, to work and play and be mischievous well into their senior years.

Jack Russells have a quiet side too, and are often happiest curled up next to the people they love.

Jack Russells tend to reflect the moods of their people. They will sit on your lap when you are resting, or curl up on a piece of your clothing to feel close to you when you are away. They will be there to comfort you when you are feeling bad, and be your four-legged shadow as you work around the house or in the garden. They are very generous with their kisses, too, and, as a high compliment, will extend those kisses to eyelids, earlobes and foreheads. The same loving behavior is, of course, also engaged in with their canine companions. Extending their muzzle as an invitation, they will spend many contented moments in such affectionate grooming activity.

Jack Russells and Children

Jack Russells do not always fare well with children— and some children do not fare well with Jack Russells. These dogs will not tolerate rough treatment. If they are abused by a child they may be inclined to discipline that child, probably quite fairly, for the offense committed. They will not put up with having their ears pulled, being stepped on or hurt in any way. They will play very hard with each other, often causing concern in those watching their practice pounces and high-pitched, mouthy battles. Children must never engage in play with Jack Russells that in any way duplicates the terriers' practice-hunting play. Even normal play within terrier circles can be serious in nature: They exert their will on each other as practice for exerting their wills on formidable quarry. Jack Russells are not suitable for small or undisciplined children and it is suggested that their time together be supervised at all times. On the other hand, JRs can be excellent with babies and considerate youngsters.

JRs can be good friends with children who know how to treat them properly.

Talkative

JRs are not "yappy," but can be very vocal when someone comes to the door. Their voices are important in their work, marking the location of their quarry while hunting below ground, so it must be understood that they are quick to express themselves this way. Some will bark when left alone for a prolonged period of time by busy families who must be gone from home. Though these dogs are small in size they are quite big at making their presence known—another trait that makes them unsuitable for close living in apartments, condos or other city dwellings.

Going for a Ride

They enjoy riding in cars, carriages or anything that moves, and have been known to jump on the backs of cross-country skis. When used in fox hunting, a JR was carried in a pouch by a terrierman on a horse and they delighted in the fast pace and jumps. They love action and being in the center of activity.

Versatile and Adaptable

JRs, with their good temperaments and love for people, can be fine companions and therapy dogs. They are intelligent, possess a wonderful sense of fun and can be loving, amusing and entertaining. They are well suited to assisting the deaf since they are attuned to such noises as buzzers and bells.

And they are adaptable. When displaced, needing a new home, they settle in quickly to any new situation where they are loved and their needs are met. They have a never-look-back attitude if their present is full of affection and mental and physical activity.

If a Jack Russell's energy and penchant for activity are boundless, so too is his capacity for affection and loyalty. The JR is at once lovable and laughable, a treasure and a trial.

Raising Your Jack Russell

WITH ANOTHER PET

Although a JR can be raised with a cat, there are many reported stories of these friendships going wrong later when the two animals are left alone and unattended. Jack Russells have been bred to have the courage to stand up to a fox, and if a fox is not available a cat may do. It is just not a good idea to keep JRs with cats, birds or pet rodents of any kind.

WITH VISITORS

After thoroughly screening a visitor, some Russells will seem to smile and throw themselves at the person's feet waiting to be petted, but they can also show a fierce side when protecting their people and territory. A Jack Russell must never be allowed to believe he has a dominant position in "his family," his "pack." His owners must be consistent in showing strong leadership. The dog can become a tyrant if he is allowed to manipulate his people. JRs need and respect the firm, fair administration of authority.

Notwithstanding the shenanigans of those terriers who are allowed to exhibit their natural tendencies to be their own masters, it is also quite natural for the majority of JRs to have a good temperament. It is very important that a puppy be well socialized early to ensure that he grows into a stable, happy, well-adjusted dog. The breed standard describes shyness (not to be confused with sensitivity) and overaggression as serious faults. Aggressive behavior toward people or other dogs should never be tolerated, and corrective training and strong guidance are required to eliminate this trait. Good temperament is vital. They should always appear confident and have happy dispositions, and they should know that they can look to their owners for guidance and love.

Training Your Jack Russell

Training Jack Russell Terriers can sometimes be a challenge. They will be brilliantly responsive, perfectly performing a task, and then start to yawn in total disinterest. They can be stubborn to the point of distraction. Harsh forms of training are cruel and never successful with Jack Russells. They do respond well to the tried and true methods of praise, reward, consistency—and good timing. If the training is too much of a boring drill, repeated over and over for too long a time, results will be disappointing. A JR just will not allow himself to become a robot. These dogs bore easily and, if bored, will sulk. The very same dog that consistently wins at obedience may turn a deaf ear to a recall if something more interesting begs his attention. The dog must perceive a purpose in the training and must enjoy himself in the process. If the activity is kept stimulating, many JRs excel at and really enjoy obedience and agility competition.

CHARACTERISTICS OF THE JACK RUSSELL TERRIER

Extremely energetic

Independent

Needs supervision with small children

Strong hunting instincts

Intelligent

Willful

Fun and Games

The Jack Russell Terrier is not an American Kennel Club (AKC) breed and cannot compete in activities sponsored by the AKC. However, the Jack Russell Terrier Club of America hosts trials across the United States that include many different activities particularly suited to Jack Russells.

Jack Russells enjoy activities such as obedience, agility, fly ball and racing. Obedience, agility and fly ball classes are offered in many areas, and competition in these events, along with racing and go-to-ground, is offered at Jack Russell Terrier Trials throughout the country.

Sanctioned trials offer competition in conformation, obedience and agility classes and certificates for achievement.

Conformation Jack Russell conformation competitions are like other dog shows. Dogs are judged on their appearance— structure, movement and temperament. The winner is the dog who comes closest to the breed standard. The Jack Russell Terrier standard is a broad one, designed to preserve these dogs as *working terriers*. In conformation competition, the winning dog must not only be pleasing to the eye, but must be a functional terrier, one who can do a job and do it well.

Jack Russells rode with hunters on their horses, and still enjoy riding on just about anything that moves.

Racing In "on the flat" races, the terriers run on a straight course for speed. In "steeplechase" competitions, small fences are placed along the racetrack and a successful finish requires agility and alertness as well. In "muskrat" races the starting box is placed at the bank of a pond and the terriers follow a floating lure to the other side of the pond. Human rescue teams are available to rescue any terriers having a hard time in the water.

Puissance Jumping   There are also high jump or puissance jumping contests which are limited to dogs over one year of age due to the stressful nature of the competition. Terriers are released from 20 feet away and are coaxed over the bar by a lure. The bar is raised in three to four inch increments. The highest jump wins!

*Jack Russells
have a great
capacity for
mastering skills
and competing
in organized
activities. These
are racing in the
1995 JRTCA
National Trial.*

Trailing and Locating   Jack Russells can also compete at trailing and locating, which simulates hunting. The terriers are timed and given points for accuracy as they follow a line of scent to a finishing point.

Go-to-Ground   In the go-to-ground competition the dog follows a safe, manmade tunnel with ninety-degree turns to locate safely caged rats (who usually sleep throughout the barking). The dogs are timed going through the tunnels and working the quarry. They love it and can burn through in lightning times.

There are different levels of performance in the go-to-ground competition: in Novice classes the dogs go through a ten foot earth with one 90-degree turn. In the Open and Certificate classes they encounter a thirty-foot earth with three 90-degree turns in the dark. The Open and Certificate dogs must "work" the quarry for a minute and the Novice must work it for thirty seconds. Working is defined as barking, scratching, lunging or even staring. The purpose of the exercise is to give the dog and handler the confidence and experience to work as a team. It is considered training for future work in natural settings in the field.

Other Activities

Jack Russells have been trained successfully to aid the hearing-impaired. Their great sense of smell and inexhaustible energy has made them indispensable as search-and-rescue dogs in disaster situations. However, they can never be trusted to lead the blind, as their Gary Larson sort of nature would probably lead their ward to the nearest freeway!

For more information on this and other activities for your Jack Russell, call the Jack Russell Terrier Club of America or some of the other organizations listed in Chapter 13, Resources.

Welcome to
the World
of the Jack
Russell Terrier

MORE INFORMATION ON THE JACK RUSSELL TERRIER

NATIONAL BREED CLUB

The Jack Russell Terrier Club of America
P.O. Box 4527
Lutherville, MD 21094-4527

The club can provide you with information on all aspects of the breed, as well as the Russell Rescue contact nearest you. Inquire about membership.

MAGAZINE

True Grit
The Official Publication of the Jack Russell Terrier
Club of America
P.O. Box 4527
Lutherville, MD 21094-4527

BOOKS

Atter, Sheila. *The Jack Russell Terrier Today.* New York: Howell Book House, 1995.

Hobson, Jeremy. *Working Terriers: Management and Training.* New York: Howell Book House, 1989.

James, Kenneth. *Working Jack Russell Terriers: A Hunter's Story.* Claremont, CA: Hunter House Press, 1995.

Lent, Patricia Adams. *Sport with Terriers.* New York: Arner Publications, 1973.

Massey, Marilyn. *Above and Below Ground.* Woodluck Publications, 1985.

Plummer, Brian D. *The Complete Jack Russell Terrier.* New York: Howell Book House, 1993.

Some of the above titles may be out of print. Check a library or a used book store for a copy.

WORLD WIDE WEB

If you have access to the Web, check out these sites for up-to-the-minute information on the Jack Russell Terrier.

http://rock.west.ora.com/~steph/Dogs/jrtfaq.html

http://rock.west.ora.com/~steph/Dogs/terror/html

http://www.pbs.org/wishbone/factsaboutjrt.html

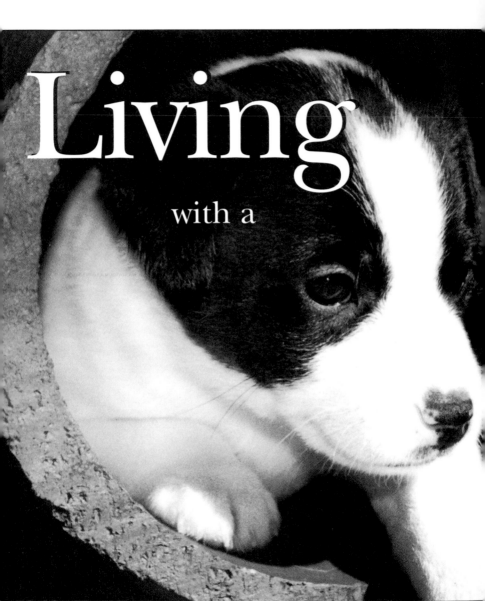

Living

with a

part two

Jack Russell Terrier

chapter 4

Bringing Your
Jack Russell
Terrier
Home

With preparation and planning, the arrival in your home of your puppy or adult dog will be a happy event. Jack Russells adjust very quickly to new situations and adapt themselves nicely to a new home.

When possible, visit your new puppy a time or two before bringing him home. (Check with the breeder first regarding his or her policy about visitors before the pups have had their first protective inoculations.) It is also good to meet the dam (mother) and the sire (father) to give you a better understanding of the personality and characteristics your dog may have. A good disposition is an important quality.

For the first few days, try to keep visitors and activities to a minimum. Give your new family member a bit of time to become acclimated to his people and his surroundings. Christmas is *not* a good time to get a new puppy or adult dog. Your schedule is busy, activity levels are high and added dangers lurk in bright, hanging ornaments and possibly toxic decorations.

Equipment

Rather than forget something, or have to settle for what you don't really like, take your time shopping and have your new puppy's supplies ready.

Puppies need lots of sleep, and a comfortable bed with a friend is an unbeatable combination.

CRATE

You will need a crate, of course, with a pad and bedding inside. You might also want to get another small bed for use outside of the crate. Jack Russells love their beds (and yours, too) and a particularly appealing one for them is a cup type made of sturdy, plush, washable material. Puppies need a lot of sleep, and snuggling into a comfy soft bed will give them the support and feeling of security they need to sleep well.

FOOD BOWLS

Sturdy crock bowls for food and water are very good for terriers. They are difficult to tip over and difficult for your puppy to pick up and carry off to who-knows-where.

LEASH AND COLLAR

You will need a leash and a collar or collars that fit properly at all stages of growth. Rolled leather collars work very well and are comfortable. Be certain to adjust the collar so that it fits securely but not tightly, and check it on a regular basis, particularly as your puppy grows. (The collar should be snug enough that it will not slip over the head, but loose enough to allow you to comfortably insert two or three fingers between the collar and the neck.)

A nylon leash may be best for puppies, who find great joy in chewing leather leashes. Make sure the clip is a sturdy one that will not release accidentally. A leather leash is recommended for JRs past the teething stage. Another item that has become very popular is a retracting leash

Jack Russells need to be on a leash when otherwise unconfined.

which extends to sixteen feet, allowing your dog to run and play more actively than is possible with a standard six-foot leash. The leash should not be a substitute for a regular leash, but it can provide a lot of fun for your dog in an open area where it can run without having to be let loose.

Puppy-Proofing Your Home

With a new terrier in your home, you will need to do some thorough puppy-proofing. A good puppy-proofing rule of thumb is to take the same precautions to protect your new puppy or dog as you would to protect an agile, inquisitive toddler, and then some. Potted plants within reach of your JR, for example, provide an ideal place to practice a skill that comes naturally to him: digging. Worse than the inconvenience of an upended plant, though, is the fact that many common houseplants and garden plants can be deadly to your dog if ingested.

Of course, medicines also must be kept out of reach of your terrier. (For a JR, out-of-reach places do not include tables or countertops.) The rattle of a bottle of pills is enticing and that bottle can easily become a toy that will spill contents that can quickly poison your dog.

And don't forget to put away the chocolates: chocolate candy, chocolate cookies and cakes, chocolate drink mixes—all of it. Dogs love the taste as much as people do; unfortunately, a dog can be poisoned after eating what would seem to us to be just a little bit of chocolate—the darker the chocolate, the more potent it is.

Remember that a very small amount of toxin can have a big impact on a small dog. Household chemicals and cleaning supplies should be secured out of reach of your dog (they can open unlatched cabinets, you know), and don't overlook all the things stored in the garage or spilled on the garage floor. Antifreeze has a pleasant taste to dogs and lapping up just a little bit can prove fatal.

Puppies, and especially Jack Russells, are very inquisitive and energetic. Puppy-proof your home to make sure it's a safe place.

Limiting the area in which your pup is allowed to roam will make house training considerably easier. Gates provide good barriers between rooms and a crate is an invaluable tool for the protection and well-being of your dog.

Crate Training

Jack Russells love their crates and use them as dens. When the door is left open and there is a comfortable bed inside, the dog will seek it by choice for privacy and rest. Either a wire crate or an airline carrier is suitable, as long as it is large enough for a grown terrier to stand up in and turn around comfortably. If the crate is too large the dog may choose to sleep at one end and eliminate at the other. The bed or pad inside should be one that is not easily torn. An added baby blanket will let a puppy snuggle in and help provide warmth and protection from drafts, especially in cold weather. A crate should not be used for more than a few hours at a time and should never be used for punishment. The crate should be a safe and happy place for your dog—a place where he will go willingly, whether you put him there or he goes in of his own accord.

Where you place the crate in your home is important for your dog's comfort. Keep it out of drafts and direct sunlight (for a wire crate, a sheet or blanket can be used as a cover for privacy and draft protection, and removed when not needed). It is also very important that the crate be in a "people area," not in a place where the dog will be isolated from his family.

Choose a time to start training when the dog is ready for rest, after he has relieved himself and has had plenty of exercise. Begin by placing a piece of kibble in the crate so your dog will enter willingly and, in a cheerful tone of voice, use a command such as "kennel" or "crate."

At first, keep the door open when the dog is inside. Then, after acclimating the dog to the crate with the door open, close the door for a few minutes. Gradually increase the time that the door is closed and practice leaving and returning to the room without any fuss. This matter-of-fact attitude helps to avoid separation

HOUSEHOLD DANGERS

Curious puppies and inquisitive dogs get into trouble not because they are bad, but simply because they want to investigate the world around them. It's our job to protect our dogs from harmful substances, like the following:

IN THE HOUSE

cleaners, especially pine oil

perfumes, colognes, aftershaves

medications, vitamins

office and craft supplies

electric cords

chicken or turkey bones

chocolate

some house and garden plants, like ivy, oleander and poinsettia

IN THE GARAGE

antifreeze

garden supplies, like snail and slug bait, pesticides, fertilizers, mouse and rat poisons anxiety later on. Your comings and goings should never be a big event with apologetic departures or excited greetings. Any vocal protest by the dog should be met with a sharp "No!" Allow the dog out only after he has settled down and has accepted containment.

Using a crate also makes housebreaking a puppy much easier. First thing in the morning (about 7:00 A.M.), immediately carry the puppy from his crate to the outdoors where he can eliminate. Then bring him in for some play time and breakfast. Shortly after breakfast, take him outside again. After another half hour or so of play time, he should be ready to go back in the crate for a nap.

Around noon, carry the pup outside, bring him in for his second meal, and repeat the above routine. Repeat the schedule again around a night meal served at about 5:00 P.M. After taking the pup from his crate and outside at about 8:30 P.M., he should be able to stay inside with you until he is taken out for the last time and then put in his crate for the night at about 11:00 P.M. No late food or drink should be offered, except for a small biscuit or two in the crate for overnight. The puppy also should have special, sturdy toys in the crate with him during the times he is contained.

This schedule is for the young, untrained pup and should be followed for no more than seven days. Your JR wants to please you and will do his best to make you proud. The dog will probably succeed within the week but, even if he is not completely trained, he will be well on his way. Above all, remember to praise, praise, praise your puppy for his successes, with only a mild correction for his mistakes. And there will be mistakes. A puppy in a new home with new people may very well eliminate in his crate. You should check often and keep the bedding scrupulously clean at all times. The problem won't last long.

Last, but not least, a crate is a must for traveling with your dog, keeping both you and the dog happier and safer. The crate also makes it more likely that you will be welcome when visiting friends and relatives on those occasions when you just can't bear to leave your pup at home. It is his familiar home away from home and he will be contented being able to see his favorite people. A Jack Russell thrives on being included in his master's activities, and his crate will make him a more welcome guest wherever he goes.

One caution should be noted: Collars with tags should be removed before crating the dog. Tags can become caught in the crate and the dog can be injured or strangled.

Activity

A Jack Russell Terrier is a body in motion; these dogs need exercise throughout their entire lives. Even in their senior years, they still tend to act like puppies—they just take longer naps!

Jack Russells are inclined to explore their surroundings and beyond at an early age.

Russell puppies will follow closely at your heels, even to the point of getting stepped on. They will wiggle when you hold them and, being as strong as they are, may wiggle right out of your grasp. Fearless by nature, they will launch themselves from dangerous (from a pup's

point of view) heights, and must never be left where they can fall from chairs or sofas and be injured.

Physical and mental needs of the Jack Russell can be met in good part by making sure the dog has adequate exercise. Dedicate part of each day to taking your terrier on long walks. Playing ball may be good exercise, too, but a brisk walk goes a much longer way in meeting the needs of the dog. It would be ideal to have a safe place in the country, away from cars, where the terrier can run to his heart's content under the watchful eyes of his owner. It is not easy to tire JRs. Their need for activity cannot be compromised and many behavioral problems can be alleviated by increased exercise.

Identification

Identification tags are easily lost and any collar can be removed. When hunting, adult working terriers' collars are removed for fear they might get caught on roots below ground. Other means of identification are much more reliable. Many dogs are tattooed on the inner thigh with an ID number (i.e., the owner's Social Security number), which is registered with a reliable system like the National Dog Registry. Because of the structure of their skin, the tattooing process is painless to dogs. Other owners prefer to have a microchip implanted beneath the dog's skin. Whatever system is used, the benefits of positive identification are immeasurable. Many dogs who would otherwise have been lost to their owners have found their way home because they were able to be positively identified.

Even at an early age, JRs are inclined to explore in search of adventure whether or not you are with them. One evening our three-month-old puppy was allowed to go along with us on a walk around the farm with our pack of terriers. At the edge of the hayfield, she vanished from sight. The little pup had managed to travel quite a distance into the fields of the next farm before signaling her distress with very vocal cries. Needless to say, she was coupled with her dam on future walks and was not allowed to fly solo again. It's easy to see why identification is so necessary for the adventurous and independent Jack Russell.

Routine

A routine is helpful to all dogs. Upon rising, they need to relieve themselves and play, then go back to rest some more. After their morning nap, they are ready for more play and exercise, and then their afternoon nap. If you work at home, you have an ideal companion. If you work away from home, it is best if you can

**PUPPY
ESSENTIALS**

Your new
puppy will
need:

food bowl

water bowl

collar

leash

I.D. tag

bed

crate

toys

grooming
supplies

get back midday to spend some time with the dog, letting him out and playing with him. If your dog must be alone during the day, leave a radio on to keep him company and use gates to confine him to one or two rooms, but don't leave him by himself for too many hours, and never leave him crated for more than a few hours at a time. This is especially hard for puppies, who may feel they are being punished or abandoned.

Perhaps a friend or neighbor can help by spending some time with the dog in the early afternoon as JRs really do cherish companionship. If you have no alternative but to be gone all day, and no one to help, you might want to consider waiting and getting a dog or puppy at a later time in your life. When you get home, take the dog outside immediately and later, after feeding and watering, take him on a long evening walk.

Toys provide stimulation for Jack Russells of all ages.

Toys

Jack Russells love toys, and appropriate ones are necessary for all stages of their lives. Hard rubber or nylon toys are best, but soft rubber squeaky toys are not at all suitable. They are easily torn apart and the squeaker is small enough for the dog to choke on. The soft rubber usually ends up shredded and swallowed.

Hard rubber balls are always a favorite and the ones with a channel cut through them are easy for little mouths to carry. Rope toys with hard rubber chew areas are very suitable and come in many shapes and sizes. Large, tightly rolled pieces of rawhide may be acceptable, but avoid smaller pieces that can be chewed down into bits and choke the dog. Also avoid rawhide with knotted ends for the same reason. Some Jack Russell breeders do not feel that rawhide of any kind is appropriate for their dogs.

By providing your JR with proper, tough, terrier-safe toys you can help to avoid damage to furniture and furnishings. Never allow your puppy or dog to chew on anything that is not meant for that activity, and always be ready to provide him with a good toy as a substitute for whatever forbidden item might be in his mouth. In distracting the puppy from such negative behavior, be sure to praise him for accepting the substitution.

Consider enrolling in an obedience class with your Jack Russell. The training and communication that you build together will strengthen your relationship and help to establish you as his pack leader. For more information on activities you can try with your Jack Russell, see Chapter 3.

Bringing Home an Adult Dog

In this chapter we have been focusing on bringing a Jack Russell into your home as a puppy, but this is not the only option. Consider getting an older, already spayed or neutered Jack Russell as companion to your dog—or as your only dog, for that matter. Many healthy, well-behaved older JRs are in need of new homes and can be applied for through the JRTCA's Russell Rescue (see page 38 for the address).

An older dog entering your home and life for the first time will have different needs than a puppy. A new puppy adjusts easily and is more adaptable, but an older dog has a history and habits, and may be more cautious in his new surroundings. The best thing you can do is to make the homecoming as stress-free as possible, and make your home a comfortable, stable environment in which your new dog will feel secure.

If you get a re-homed dog from a rescue group or other source, you may not know much about the dog's history. The more you can find out, the better prepared you will be for the task ahead. Unfortunately, some rescue dogs have been harmed at the hands of humans, and will have to be patiently taught to love and trust again.

You can make this easier by being sensitive to the special circumstances of your JR. Notice anything that seems to make him uncomfortable. Avoid movements or noises that seem to scare him. Introduce children to your new JR in as calm a manner as possible. Don't let them jump on him or make loud, excited noises that may startle or frighten him.

If you have another pet in the house, make sure their introduction and interactions are supervised, especially at first. It's best to introduce them outside on neutral territory, leashed of course. As they become more comfortable with each other, let them out together, but stay close. Do not leave them unsupervised until you are sure they have accepted each other.

Take your dog for long walks around your neighborhood to let him get his bearings and familiarize himself with his new environment. The sooner he feels at home, the better.

An older JR should adjust quickly to your home and lifestyle. They are "no-regrets" dogs. With patience and understanding he will soon be his happy, eager JR self. You can be proud you have offered him a second chance and a wonderful new home.

chapter 5

Feeding
Your
Jack Russell
Terrier

People have different opinions on the proper feeding of Jack Russell Terriers. All agree, however, that good nutrition is essential to good health, and that the nutritional needs of the dog change throughout life.

Feeding Your Jack Russell Puppy

Having started life on the dam's milk, puppies are weaned between five and six weeks of age. The timing depends on the dam's willingness to nurse and the practices of the breeder. While the pups are still nursing, at about four weeks, the breeder will begin to feed them a fine-textured, well-moistened, nutritious gruel to begin to acclimate them to solid food. At first the food is all over the place. It must be served in a low dish or pan so they can reach it, but then, of course, they can also walk and play in it. This milestone in the puppies' lives marks the beginning of several weeks of more cleanup work for the breeder.

Puppies should never leave their dam and littermates before they are fully eight weeks of age, and by the time you bring your puppy home he will have been fully weaned and eagerly crunching on puppy kibble. The breeder should send you home with a supply of the food that the pup has been eating. You can either continue feeding that food or change to a different one. If you change, do it gradually, starting with about 25 percent of the new food, increasing the proportion for about a week until only the new food is being served. Changing food for dogs of any age should be done in this manner to avoid upsetting the puppy's or dog's digestive system.

Before you even bring your puppy home, your breeder will have introduced it to fine gruel, and later to puppy kibble.

Young puppies should be fed three times a day, at about the same times each day, one-third of the daily ration at each serving. Offer the food to the pup and allow him to eat for ten or fifteen minutes. At the end of that time, pick up the dish and do not offer more food until the next mealtime. You probably won't have to worry about your Jack Russell puppy eating enough—most are eager eaters. They may play around or even miss a meal or two, particularly when they are first brought to their new home, but they will soon get with the program. (A loss of appetite for longer periods may require your veterinarian's attention.) Be very sure that plenty of fresh, clean water is always available.

Puppies require more protein and calories per pound of body weight than adults, so a general rule of thumb for Jack Russells is to serve the same amount of food per day to a pup as you would expect him to eat each day as an adult. For the most part, this would be about one cup of good-quality, small kibble per day. You can check with the breeder for information on how much food he or she expects your pup will require as an adult. Feeding guidelines printed on dog-food bags are only estimates and should not be relied on as the precise amounts to feed your dog or puppy.

When your puppy reaches five or six months of age he can be fed just twice a day, morning and evening, one-half the daily ration each. Many breeders continue to feed two meals a day throughout the life of the dog, but some choose to feed only once a day after the dog reaches adulthood.

Feeding the Older Jack Russell

Jack Russells remain quite active well into their senior years. However, compared to the levels they maintained as youngsters, even these lively terriers tend to slow down and nap more as they age, perhaps gaining some weight in the process.

When JRs get to be more than six years old they may require fewer calories (particularly if they are gaining some weight) while still needing all of the essential nutritional elements found in a well-balanced food. As the digestive system and absorption of nutrients also slow down a bit, you may want to feed your senior JR smaller, more frequent meals.

TYPES OF FOODS/TREATS

There are three types of commercially available dog food—dry, canned and semimoist—and a huge assortment of treats (lucky dogs!) to feed your dog. Which should you choose?

Dry and canned foods contain similar ingredients. The primary difference between them is their moisture content. The moisture is not just water. It's blood and broth, too, the very things that dogs adore. So while canned food is more palatable, dry food is more economical, convenient and effective in controlling tartar buildup. Most owners feed a 25% canned/75% dry diet to give their dogs the benefit of both. Just be sure your dog is getting the nutrition he needs (you and your veterinarian can determine this).

Semimoist foods have the flavor dogs love and the convenience owners want. However, they tend to contain excessive amounts of artificial colors and preservatives.

Dog treats come in every size, shape and flavor imaginable, from organic cookies shaped like postmen to beefy chew sticks. Dogs seem to love them all, so enjoy the variety. Just be sure not to overindulge your dog. Factor treats into her regular meal sizes.

Feeding More than One JR

If you are feeding more than one puppy or dog, it is best to keep them separated, preferably serving them in their individual crates. That way, you will avoid conflict and you can be sure that each dog gets to eat his full portion. Remove any food that has not been eaten within ten or fifteen minutes.

Free Feeding?

"Free feeding," (keeping food available to your dog at all times) is not recommended for Jack Russells—it

is just too tempting. A fat Jack Russell is not desired, nor is he healthy. JRs should always appear fit and be in good working condition. All calories do count. Be sure to include biscuits and treats when calculating your dog's total daily intake. A good, quick way to determine if your terrier is carrying too much fat is to put your hand over his back, thumb on one side, fingers on the other, and run your hand lightly down the back. You should be able to feel the individual ribs, but you should not be able to see them.

Puppies and dogs with a high activity level need about 25 or 26 percent protein in their diets.

What to Feed Your JR

Dry food, or primarily dry food, is recommended. With the kibble, some warm water may be added to release more food odors. Canned foods are not always necessary but, if you feel you must add it, take care that it does not exceed 20 or 25 percent of the dog's diet. A puppy raised on dry food, with or without the occasional addition of water, will be quite content with that food for his lifetime. To help keep your dog's teeth and gums healthy, do avoid semimoist food (which has a lot of salt, sugar and preservatives) and too much canned food. These soft preparations encourage tartar buildup, which can lead to periodontal disease. Hard kibble helps to keep teeth clean and gums healthy.

There are so many brands and types of dog food, it can be difficult to decide what is best for your Jack Russell. Premium food of high quality should always be chosen over less expensive food that may contain fillers and artificial colors and additives.

The dog's stool is a primary indicator of the digestibility (usable amount of nutrients) of the food he is eating. The lower-cost food may be a soy- or corn-based product, which tends to cause a larger, looser stool. Listed on the bag in descending order of quantity, the first ingredient listed in higher-quality foods is a meat product, with grains following after, resulting in a denser, well-formed stool.

Although store and discount brands should probably be avoided, relatively low-cost, high-quality foods are still available in both grocery and feed stores. Read and compare labels, seek quality and palatability and you can be sure that you will be providing the best food available for your terrier.

PROTEIN

One area of canine nutrition debate involves protein. Some still believe that if some is good, more is better—particularly for puppies, and bitches in whelp or lactating.

> ## HOW TO READ THE DOG FOOD LABEL
>
> With so many choices on the market, how can you be sure you are feeding the right food for your dog? The information is all there on the label—if you know what you're looking for.
>
> Look for the nutritional claim right up top. Is the food "100% nutritionally complete"? If so, it's for nearly all life stages; "growth and maintenance," on the other hand, is for early development; puppy foods are marked as such, as are foods for senior dogs.
>
> Ingredients are listed in descending order by weight. The first three or four ingredients will tell you the bulk of what the food contains. Look for the highest-quality ingredients, like meats and grains, to be among them.
>
> The Guaranteed Analysis tells you what levels of protein, fat, fiber and moisture are in the food, in that order. While these numbers are meaningful, they won't tell you much about the quality of the food. Nutritional value is in the dry matter, not the moisture content.
>
> In many ways, seeing is believing. If your dog has bright eyes, a shiny coat, a good appetite and a good energy level, chances are his diet's fine. Your dog's breeder and your veterinarian are good sources of advice if you're still confused.

But high concentrations of protein in a dog's diet are believed to be hard on the kidneys, especially for older dogs or dogs with a history of kidney problems. Working dogs and puppies may be fed food with protein levels of 25 or 26 percent; mature dogs fare well with a level of 20 percent.

FAT

Another consideration is the fat content of dog food. Owners of working dogs and dogs housed in outdoor kennels in cold weather may prefer a higher fat content, maybe 15 percent. Dogs, and even puppies, who are housed indoors, and older and overweight dogs, will probably do very well on a food with a fat content of around 10 percent.

SUPPLEMENTS

One more consideration is supplements. Don't give them unless they are prescribed by your veterinarian for some special reason. All good-quality dog foods labeled as "complete" will provide all that your dog needs in the way of nutrition. There may be rare or special circumstances, such as pregnancy and lactation, when your dog may require some supplementation of one or more nutrients, if recommended by your veterinarian. But casual supplementation can cause serious imbalances and unexpected problems. More of a good thing is not necessarily better.

HOW MANY MEALS A DAY?

Individual dogs vary in how much they should eat to maintain a desired body weight—not too fat, but not too thin. Puppies need several meals a day, while older dogs may need only one. Determine how much food keeps your adult dog looking and feeling her best. Then decide how many meals you want to feed with that amount. Like us, most dogs love to eat, and offering two meals a day is more enjoyable for them. If you're worried about overfeeding, make sure you measure correctly and abstain from adding tidbits to the meals.

Whether you feed one or two meals, only leave your dog's food out for the amount of time it takes her to eat it—10 minutes, for example. Freefeeding (when food is available any time) and leisurely meals encourage picky eating. Don't worry if your dog doesn't finish all her dinner in the allotted time. She'll learn she should.

Basically, the food you serve your Jack Russell Terrier should contain protein, fat, carbohydrates, fiber, vitamins and minerals, all in proper quantities and in proper proportion to each other. It is highly unlikely that the quality food you purchase at your grocery or feed store will be lacking in any nutrient your dog needs for healthy growth, development and maintenance.

It is impossible to give general advice and be right all the time. You know your terrier better than anyone else. As a responsible pet owner, you should seek the advice of your veterinarian and breeder, read labels and then decide what food is best. The appearance of your dog is the best indicator of good nutrition; watch him as he develops, grows and ages, and adjust accordingly.

SNACKS

Just like adding artificial colors to dog food, and continually switching brands as all those ads encourage you to do, the feeding of table scraps does more to please people than to benefit dogs. Your dog doesn't care about all those colors; he's perfectly happy with that plain old high-quality kibble he's always eaten, and if you never feed him table scraps, he'll never know what he's missed. Scraps tend to be full of fat, salt, sugar and spices—nothing that's needed by or is good for your dog. Even if you feed something healthful from the table, the dog will still get into the habit of begging, which will become a mealtime annoyance forever—not to mention the fact that your terrier could end up being a very finicky eater.

> **TO SUPPLEMENT OR NOT TO SUPPLEMENT?**
>
> If you're feeding your dog a diet that's correct for her developmental stage and she's alert, healthy-looking and neither over- nor underweight, you don't need to add supplements. These include table scraps as well as vitamins and minerals. In fact, a growing puppy is in danger of developing musculoskeletal disorders by oversupplementation. If you have any concerns about the nutritional quality of the food you're feeding, discuss them with your veterinarian.

Good "people food" snacks for your terrier, in moderation, are pieces of carrot or apple. Most JRs love them. Offer the snack between meals—yours and the dog's—or as rewards in training sessions.

chapter 6

Grooming
Your
Jack Russell
Terrier

The Jack Russell Terrier is considered a "no-frills" working terrier, but even working terriers need their coats maintained to keep them efficient and clean. Weekly maintenance of the Jack Russell's coat also will provide a perfect opportunity to give your dog a very good going-over to see that all is in order, and you'll get some quality bonding time as well.

The JR is a double-coated breed that is seen in three varieties. The smooth should have a dense undercoat with a harsh overcoat that will protect it from the elements and underbrush. The rough-coated JR should have a very dense undercoat with an extremely coarse overcoat to protect it from the elements. The broken coat has elements of the rough and smooth.

Smooth coats shed more freely than the rough or broken coats, but all coat types shed continuously. The hairs work into fabrics and can be difficult to remove. If you are uncomfortable finding white hairs, year round, on your clothing and furniture, be warned that this is unavoidable with a Jack Russell in your household.

Supplies

Items that you will need to groom your terrier are:

rubber hound glove

trimmer knife

horsehair glove

greyhound comb

flea comb

nail trimmer

grooming stone

magnet cloth

McClellan knives, fine and coarse

tooth scaler

tooth thinning shears

finger toothbrush and paste

straight shears

styptic powder

To begin the care of your dog, place him on a table of a height that will make the dog accessible to work with and that is comfortable for your back. Ideally, you will have a noose to restrain the dog so that both of your hands will be free for grooming. *Never leave the dog unattended while he is restrained in the noose.* If you must stop the procedure, have a crate ready in which to place the dog until you return.

Grooming Your Smooth-Coated JR

For a smooth-coated terrier, start with a thorough, all-over brushing, followed by a rubdown with a well soaked, tightly squeezed magnet cloth. This removes old hair and debris, giving a nice fresh look to the coat. Then look the dog over for anything that may need attention: teeth, eyes, nails, injury to foot pads, fleas and ticks, an unusual smell in the ears, and so forth (see Chapter 7). (Any unusual smell or matter in the ears requires the attention of a veterinarian.)

In between this weekly schedule, you will want to brush the dog almost daily because of the free-shedding tendency of the smooth coat.

Grooming Your Rough- or Broken-Coated Jack Russell

Rough- or broken-coated terriers require a bit more work. Left to their own devices, they would not receive a "Tidy Terrier" award. Though grooming the roughs or brokens is more involved, you may receive more satisfaction with the finished product.

Begin the grooming of a rough or broken by thoroughly combing and brushing the dog to loosen dead hair and dirt. Then step back and decide whether or not the dog needs to be stripped of accumulated dead hair. If you decide to strip and build a "jacket" on the terrier, you will use your McClellan knives (which you will have first dulled by running them over an old brick), to remove the offending growth. Longer hairs are removed with the coarse knife, in small amounts, with a straight pull, not bending your wrist. Always pull in the direction in which the hair grows. Begin at the head and proceed to the neck and shoulders, then the back and thighs, ending with the sides.

When all the long hair has been pulled, and your dog looks like he is in his underwear, you can let him rest a bit while you trim his nails, remove unwanted hair from between the toes, and generally check him all over as described above. When this grooming procedure has been completed, mark the date on a calendar and circle the date ten days from then. On the tenth day, "rake" out the undercoat with the trimmer knife, which is used only for raking and never for stripping. (Do not dull the stripper as you did the McClellan knives.) This is a sharp instrument, so be very careful not to dig into the coat.

Now that the basic coat work is done, you will begin daily maintenance. Put the dog up on the table and, with your rubber hound glove on one hand and your horsehair glove on the other, alternately stroke the dog with each hand for five minutes. This soon becomes a favored procedure for the terrier and, again, gives you an opportunity to examine him. After the "gloving" has been completed, selectively pluck the individual long hairs that will be sticking up. At this point, you will find that there will be a fair number of such long hairs but, as the days go by and the plucking continues, the "jacket" becomes tighter and there will be fewer and fewer hairs that stick out.

Grooming the rough- or broken-coated Jack Russell is admittedly more work, but the results are worth the effort.

Every week during the grooming session, "rake" the coat to remove excess undercoat. If this is not done, the top coat will begin to lift and start to look like a hay field gone by. The terrier will appear very untidy.

The coat of the Jack Russell is never sculpted, as it should not be altered in such a manner as to give it an artificial, overdone appearance. This is a natural earth dog and should reflect that attitude. If you are exhibiting your JR, the judge will be considering the dog that best suits the standard of the working terrier and that he or she would most like to take out into the field that day. Exaggerated leg furnishings and beards are not requirements of that standard.

Bathing

Bathing a Jack Russell Terrier is not an event that is necessary in his life, unless he gets "skunked"

or rolls in something completely objectionable or has a serious flea problem. (Flea control and skunks are addressed in Chapter 7.) If a bath truly becomes necessary, be sure the ears are plugged with cotton balls and the eyes are protected from soap. Most dogs do not like baths, and the added stress of soapy eyes may make for more resistance to a bath the next time around.

The shampoo should be a harsh-coat preparation. Anything that contains a conditioner will prove detrimental to the jacket of the dog. Terrier coats are, for the most part, very harsh. Above all, be certain that all soapy

When well-groomed, the Jack Russell should never appear artificial or overdone.

residue is completely rinsed out and that the coat is thoroughly dried before the dog is returned to the outdoors. If you are bathing an aged animal, use a hair dryer to help dry the coat and keep the dog inside until it is completely dry, except for a brief time out to relieve himself.

Nails

Always try to keep a good foot on your terrier by keeping the nails well tended. If you are diligent about trimming nails, you should have no trouble maintaining a well-rounded foot. Ideally, you will have the opportunity to manicure the foot from puppyhood, thereby establishing proper ground rules and conduct.

When clipping nails, it is of the utmost importance that you work in the best light possible. You should be quite able to see the quick very clearly and not clip into it. (If a nail is black, cut it back about the same distance as the clear ones, erring on the side of less distance than more.) Please do not try to cut as close as possible to the quick in the first few times you trim your dog's nails. And if you think a nail is not short enough after you have just cut it, do not repeat the clipping on that nail. If you hurt the dog, it will be just that much harder to get the job done the next time. (Some people like to use a grinder, but good working terriers wear down their nails, which then only need minimum attention.) Should you happen to nip the nail close enough to cause the dog discomfort, quickly apply styptic powder. Then cut the next several nails longer so the dog does not get the idea that nail clippers mean pain. If you are in real doubt about foot care, it is best to have your veterinarian attend to it or assist you the first few times you do it—but do be sure that the nails are done. Nails that are too long can cause the dog to stand and move incorrectly and can harm the feet.

Clipping nails is a necessary grooming procedure.

This chapter outlines procedures for the thorough care and grooming of your terrier's coat. However, the average dog will do just as well with basic grooming, together with proper care of the nails and feet and attention to health matters.

A Jack Russell may have either a "smooth," "rough" or "broken" coat.

This may sound like a great deal of work to the novice, but after all is said and done, the Jack Russell Terrier is a wash-and-wear type of dog.

The real object is to get your hands on your dog daily or, at the very least, weekly. Doing this, you will have an opportunity to bond with your dog while giving him a thorough health inspection. Make it a really fun time for both of you. Your dog will come away looking and feeling his best and you will have the satisfaction of knowing you are taking the best possible care of him.

chapter 7

Keeping Your
Jack Russell Terrier
Healthy

Having explored the intelligence and charm and, perhaps, the not so charming attributes of the Jack Russell Terrier, it is worth noting here that the JR seems to have fewer inherited (genetic) problems than many other breeds of dogs. Most JRs can live long, healthy, happy lives when provided with safe surroundings and the exercise and close companionship they crave and demand.

Preventive Care

Most health problems are preventable! Vaccinations, a yearly health examination by your dog's veterinarian, good nutrition, adequate daily exercise and loving companionship are the most important things you can provide for your dog to keep him healthy, mentally and physically.

67

As soon as possible after you purchase your puppy or adult dog, you should take him or her to your veterinarian for a physical examination, any vaccinations that are due, a parasite check and, if necessary, worming. In addition to the pedigree and stud certificate, the breeder or previous owner should have provided you with the dog's health records, current through the date of purchase.

Make your trip to the veterinarian a pleasant one. You should not act nervous or make a fuss over the trip or any procedure, as your terrier will be sure to pick up on your feelings. Your dog's introduction to his doctor should be very matter-of-fact.

Vaccinations

Common diseases are best avoided by the schedule of preventive care suggested by your veterinarian. The first vaccinations should be given to the puppy at about five or six weeks of age when the immunity provided by the dam declines. The second set of vaccines should be at ten to twelve weeks and the third at fourteen to sixteen weeks. These inoculations will protect your dog

Vaccinations are necessary for a happy, healthy JR.

from distemper, hepatitis, leptospirosis, parvovirus and kennel cough. Given annually thereafter, they are necessary for the continued good health of your pet. The following diseases can be prevented by following the vaccination schedule set up by your veterinarian.

When your puppy reaches four to six months of age he will need his first **rabies** shot. Thereafter, rabies shots are required either every year or every third year. If there is an outbreak of deadly infectious rabies in your area, more frequent protection may either be recommended or be the rule. Rabies is a fatal disease affecting the nervous system. It is transmitted via infected saliva to humans and other animals from a bite or through a cut or scratch on the skin. Foxes, skunks, raccoons and bats can carry the virus, as can nearly all warm-blooded animals. JRs are fast to find critters during walks and it is of the utmost importance that they be kept vaccinated—for your protection as well as theirs. Among other symptoms, a change of temperament may indicate a rabies infection; dilated, light-sensitive eyes may cause the dog to seek seclusion. The animal will withdraw and show signs of aggression, lack of coordination and loss of facial muscle control. There is no effective treatment for dogs. Coma and death will follow.

Protection from **Lyme disease** is a good idea if you live in or travel with your dog to Lyme-endemic areas. This involves, first, a series of two injections given two weeks apart, then one injection annually thereafter. Lyme disease is transmitted by very small ticks carried primarily by deer and mice. An infected dog may suddenly become lame because of painful, swollen joints and may be weak and feverish. The disease may lead to heart or kidney problems and chronic arthritic conditions. Lyme disease may be difficult to diagnose but it does respond to a variety of antibiotics.

Distemper is a killer of puppies and dogs who are not vaccinated. It is easily spread from one dog to another and can become airborne. Loss of appetite, diarrhea, discharge from nose and eyes and a dry cough are symptoms of distemper. A dog who survives can suffer from permanent damage to the brain and nervous system.

Canine hepatitis may be spread by contact with infected dogs, their urine, feces or saliva. It affects the liver, kidneys and lining of the blood vessels. There will be a discharge from eyes, mouth and nose and it may be hard to distinguish hepatitis from distemper.

YOUR PUPPY'S VACCINES

Vaccines are given to prevent your dog from getting an infectious disease like canine distemper or rabies. Vaccines are the ultimate preventive medicine: they're given before your dog ever gets the disease so as to protect him from the disease. That's why it is necessary for your dog to be vaccinated routinely. Puppy vaccines start at eight weeks of age for the five-in-one DHLPP vaccine and are given every three to four weeks until the puppy is sixteen months old. Your veterinarian will put your puppy on a proper schedule and will remind you when to bring in your dog for shots.

*Squeeze eye oint-
ment into the
lower lid.*

Leptospirosis is often passed on to dogs from the urine of infected rats, and because JRs are often associated with barns and stables where rats dwell, it is wise to keep them well protected. The disease damages the liver, kidneys and digestive tract, and symptoms include pain, depression, sores in the mouth, vomiting, diarrhea and a yellow color in the eyes.

Parvovirus is a highly contagious viral disease transmitted via infected fecal matter carried on dogs' paws and hair, shoes, cages and so forth. Puppies often die of this disease. The illness may begin with loss of appetite, depression and vomiting, seriously progressing to diarrhea, often bloody, and fever. Parvo may strike in forms that damage the heart or attack the gastrointestinal tract, and may bring on congestive heart failure. Where there has been an outbreak of parvo, the dog's living space should be cleaned and disinfected with a diluted chlorine bleach solution.

Kennel cough is not fatal but does make a dog more susceptible to other infections. It is very contagious and any affected dog should be isolated. Your veterinarian will suggest antibiotics and keeping the dog in a warm and humid environment. There are several viruses that cause kennel cough, and the parainfluenza and bordetella vaccines help to prevent spreading this affliction. Kennel cough may be contracted where a number of dogs are housed or congregate in a confined environment.

Another important component of preventive care is making sure all the working parts of your working terrier are in good order. Keeping eyes, ears and teeth clean and healthy is important for maintaining a happy, healthy pet.

Ears

Ears on the Jack Russell fold over, which, in theory, is to help keep dirt out of the inner ear when they are below ground. If you see your dog shaking his head or scratching his ears, or if there is an unpleasant odor, dirt might be embedded in the ear, there may be an infection or ear mites could be present. Your veterinarian can give you a diagnosis. If mites are present, he or she will prescribe drops to eliminate them. Mites are highly contagious and all pets in the home should be checked and treated.

Inspect your dog's ears weekly to keep ahead of any problems that may arise. You may want to use a liquid ear cleansing product. Clean the ears with a cotton swab, but never go farther into the ear than you can see.

Eyes

Eye care is important, and eyes should be checked every week, or more often if the dog is working. When a Jack Russell follows his nose and instincts, he will enter an earth and probably end up with dirt or particles of sand in his eyes. If this foreign matter is not removed, the corneas may be scratched. Even nonworking dogs will often have foreign matter in their eyes. You can wash out the eyes with lukewarm water or a special eye-cleaning preparation. Pull the lids back to make sure there is no dirt hiding in the corners of the eye.

Dental care is important for dogs and should be introduced when they are young in a cheerful and painless way.

If you have to use eye drops or apply a topical ophthalmic ointment to your dog's eyes, hold his head against your chest, tip the head upward, pull down the lower eyelid and apply the medication. The Jack Russell is small enough that one person can handle this procedure rather easily. Never use medication in the dog's eyes that has not been prescribed by your veterinarian.

Teeth

Dental care is important to your dog's overall health, and brushing and scaling his teeth help promote good

71

dental health. Tartar deposits build up quickly, particularly on the back upper molars and the canines, leading to gum disease. Puppies can be trained to accept dental care if the process is done frequently. Keep the sessions upbeat and short.

There are toothbrushes designed especially for dogs, and gauze wrapped around your finger also works. Because a dog cannot spit, he will swallow the toothpaste, so please be sure to use a formulation made especially for dogs. Tooth scalers can be obtained from a canine products catalog, where you can also purchase the toothbrushes and toothpaste.

Check your dog's teeth frequently and brush them regularly.

Have your dog's teeth checked at least once a year by the veterinarian. It may sometimes be necessary for him or her to more thoroughly clean your dog's teeth, particularly if your dog is older. Your veterinarian will sedate your dog for this procedure.

Neglected teeth may lead to periodontal disease. The bacteria can enter the bloodstream and is associated with other diseases of the heart, liver and kidneys. Watch for red or bleeding gums. Bad breath is another major indication that the dog needs to visit the vet for treatment.

Anal Glands

Anal glands are the scent glands of the dog, which also provide lubrication for the passing of stools. The sacs are located on either side and slightly down from the anus. They normally empty when the dog defecates, but may have a tendency to fill in some dogs and so should be checked from time to time. When a dog scoots along the ground, it may be taken as a sign of worms but it also could be that the sacs are plugged and the dog is trying to empty them. They are irritating to the dog and make him uncomfortable. Expressing the sacs can be easily done by any JR owner.

Using a soft cloth or tissue, take the skin of the anus and pull it outward with a gentle, twisting motion. This gentle action encourages the sacs to empty. If any blood or infectious matter is seen, take your dog to the veterinarian.

Internal and External Parasites

Internal and external parasites are a continuous and potentially serious, even deadly, problem for your dog.

EXTERNAL

Ticks Various species of ticks may attach themselves to your dog, the brown dog tick being the most common. In addition to Lyme disease, ticks can also carry such ailments as Rocky Mountain spotted fever and canine ehrlichiosis. If you find only a few ticks on your dog (the most common areas where you will find ticks are the ears, neck and head and between the toes) the easiest thing to do is remove them. First, using a cotton ball or swab, dab alcohol or nail polish on the tick and wait a few moments. This should either kill the tick or at least encourage it to loosen its grip. Then with tweezers, grasp the tick as close as possible to the dog's skin and firmly and steadily pull it out. Check to make sure the head and mouth parts were removed. If not, do not be too concerned; infections from tick bites are rare. Clean the area with antiseptic and dress with an antibiotic ointment.

Use tweezers to remove ticks from your dog.

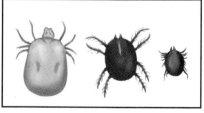

Three types of ticks (l-r): the wood tick, brown dog tick and deer tick.

Fleas These pests are a long-standing annoyance to dogs and owners. Flea "dirt" (digested dog blood) can be seen as specks in the dog's coat. If the "dirt" is moistened, it becomes a rusty red color, distinguishing it from soil. White specks that you may find on your dog are flea eggs. The saliva of the flea is very irritating, and dogs who are allergic to the saliva will break out in a rash (flea allergy dermatitis). Itching becomes so severe that, because of constant scratching and biting, hair is lost in affected areas, primarily the base of the tail, inner thighs and back of the rear legs.

Fleas flourish in a warm, humid environment. Having fallen off the dog and found a cozy place to incubate, it takes only a few days for the eggs to hatch into larvae. The larvae spin a cocoon, go into a pupal stage and, in good conditions, adult fleas will emerge in two or three weeks, though this stage can also last up to several months. After hatching, they go looking for food. They are hardy critters, however, and if they can't find any food right away, they can go without for many months. This is why it is important to rid your home as well as your dog of these parasites. As soon as your terrier walks by and provides a tasty meal, the life cycle begins once again. One female flea can lay thousands of eggs in her lifetime.

The most effective means of flea control involves breaking the life cycle. If you have a serious infestation, bathe your dog with a flea shampoo and thoroughly vacuum the floors and furniture in your home, discarding the bag outside.

There are systemic chemical agents available for flea control that are administered orally or topically. Great care must be taken in their use and the fact remains that the flea must bite the dog to be affected by these treatments. Insect growth regulators are new and relatively safe chemicals that interrupt the flea's life cycle

FIGHTING FLEAS

Remember, the fleas you see on your dog are only part of the problem—the smallest part! To rid your dog and home of fleas, you need to treat your dog *and* your home. Here's how:

• Identify where your pet(s) sleep. These are "hot spots."

• Clean your pets' bedding regularly by vacuuming and washing.

• Spray "hot spots" with a non-toxic, long-lasting flea larvicide.

• Treat outdoor "hot spots" with insecticide.

• Kill eggs on pets with a product containing insect growth regulators (IGRs).

• Kill fleas on pets per your veterinarian's recommendation.

by affecting eggs and larvae. Again, they are chemicals and the flea must still bite the dog.

Many people are concerned about using chemicals on their dogs and in their homes. They may want to consider the alternative of food-quality diatomaceous earth, which is dusted on the dog and his bedding. Diatomaceous earth is the fossilized remains of marine organisms with microscopic sharp edges that scratch the surface of the immature stages of the fleas' development, causing them to dehydrate. The food-quality diatomaceous earth is harmless to humans and animals. It is an ingestible food additive used to prevent caking in large-animal feeds.

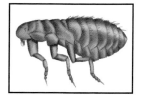

The flea is a die-hard pest.

A very effective way to safely keep fleas in check is to comb your dog every day, or almost every day, during flea season. All you will need is a fine flea comb and a glass of water into which you have mixed a few drops of mild liquid soap. When the comb picks up fleas, quickly dip it into the soapy water and remove the fleas from the comb. (The soap coats the flea and kills it.) Keep the glass close to you. If it is too far away, those critters may have time to jump off the comb.

Sarcoptic mange This condition is caused by a microscopic insect called a mite. Jack Russells love to poke around in earthen holes they discover, and if the last resident of that hole carried mange mites, the terrier may pick it up. Mange appears in many areas of the country and is especially hard on red foxes, which are often seen missing large patches of their red coat and proud brush (tail). Mange frequently shows up first on the face, ears, belly or thighs of the dog, and then spreads with itchy patches of missing hair and scabbed areas of skin. The mite feeds and reproduces on the dog, and treatment from a veterinarian is required. If your dog has mange mites, you may find that you, too, are itching. Fortunately, though, the mites cannot complete their life cycle on humans and will not last long there (provided the dog has been successfully treated).

INTERNAL

Dogs get worms! From the time the dog is born and throughout its life, controlling worms is a concern to the dog owner. When you first get your dog or puppy and take him for his first visit to your veterinarian, be sure to have with you the health records the breeder or previous owner gave to you. These records should reflect not only the vaccinations your dog has received, but also a schedule of dewormings. And also bring with you a fresh stool sample for analysis. The vet can quickly tell you what, if any, worms your dog is harboring.

Roundworms If your puppy's dam has ever had roundworms (and it is likely that she has), her pups

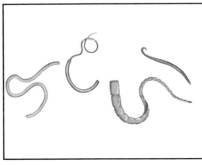

probably will be born with roundworms. Some larvae encyst in tissue and, in the late stages of pregnancy, the dormant larvae are released and carried to the unborn puppies. They are also passed on through breast milk. It is advisable to deworm a female before she is bred, but doing so will not rid her of the encysted lar-

*Common inter-
nal parasites
(l-r): roundworm,
whipworm, tape-
worm and hook-
worm.*

vae. For this reason, puppies must be dewormed by the time they are two or three weeks of age. The worms will be passed in the feces. The treatment should be repeated at least once again about two weeks later. A third, or even fourth, course of treatment may be necessary if worms are found after the previous treatment. The usual medication used against roundworms in puppies is very safe. Roundworms are not much of a problem in adults, but puppies can die from a heavy infestation.

Hookworms The same medication is also very effective against hookworms should they be present in the puppy. It is uncommon for a pup to be born with hookworms, but these parasites can be acquired through the mother's milk during the first two or three weeks of life. Left unchecked, an affected puppy can quickly die.

Whipworms These are a third type of internal parasite to be contended with. Because the female lays fewer eggs than most other worms, it can be harder to detect their presence. When whips are found, a relatively long treatment is required to eliminate them.

Tapeworm Perhaps the most familiar internal parasite for dog owners is the tapeworm. There are different kinds of tapeworm, but the most common is the one transmitted by fleas. (The flea ingests tapeworm eggs and the dog bites or swallows the flea.) Another type of tapeworm is acquired by eating animal parts, including mice. The head of the worm attaches to the wall of the gut; the body is made up of segments that contain the eggs. By the time you see segments in the feces or in the dog's hair around the anus, there is probably a fairly heavy infestation. See your veterinarian immediately.

The best method of controlling internal parasites is cleanliness. Always keep feces picked up and keep your dog free of fleas. Maintain a clean and dry environment to discourage the further development of eggs and larvae and disinfect dog areas. A solution of three cups of bleach to one gallon of water is a good disinfectant to use.

Heartworm Heartworm is very serious but can be prevented from infecting your dog. After a bite from an infected mosquito, larvae work their way into the dog and eventually develop into small adult worms. The worms then enter the bloodstream and travel to the heart, where they mature. The female gives birth to thousands of live young, called "microfilaria," which move into the bloodstream and wait for their host (the mosquito) to come along to help them develop into larvae ready to infect another dog.

Dozens of heartworms, up to twelve inches long, have been found in the heart of just one dog. There may be no symptoms of infestation for several years, and even then the early symptoms may be misinterpreted.

Prevention is vital for the safety of your dog. Blood is drawn and tested to assure that the dog is free from infection. If he is, your veterinarian will prescribe a heartworm preventive to be given in daily or monthly doses. Depending upon where you live, you may have to administer the drug year-round. In colder areas, where mosquitoes retire for the winter, you may be able to stop for a few months. Your veterinarian will tell you what procedure must be followed. The devastation caused to a dog's heart and lungs by heartworms is unimaginable and unnecessary. Responsible pet owners will not hesitate to initiate a regimen of prevention for the life of their pets.

Other, different types of parasites may trouble your dog. Known as protozoans, they are one-celled animals, invisible to the naked eye, that invade the intestinal tract. Again, unsanitary, overcrowded conditions are the usual cause. The primary symptom is diarrhea, which may affect puppies more seriously and quickly than adults. Your veterinarian must be consulted; diagnosis can be confirmed through fecal tests.

Please do not think that over-the-counter remedies for parasites will work properly. Only your dog's doctor is qualified to diagnose, treat and prescribe for parasitic infestations. Self-medication can cause you to lose precious time your vet may need to help your dog or puppy—or even save its life.

First-Aid Situations

BITES AND STINGS

Insect stings are annoying, cause swelling and may bring on allergic reactions in some terriers. Multiple stings may cause shock. Your veterinarian will instruct you on the treatment required for insect stings, and perhaps suggest an antihistamine to control swelling. Watch the site for any signs of possible infection.

The call of the wild is irresistible to Jack Russells. On any given day, while walking in the woods, your JR may find himself face to face with some form of wildlife. A groundhog bite heals quickly and rarely infects, but an encounter with a raccoon is a more serious matter.

Raccoons may carry rabies or coonhound paralysis and they have been known to drown even large dogs if they are near a body of water. Raccoons that are seen during daylight hours are probably sick. They should be avoided at all costs.

Skunks are to be avoided also, and not just for the obvious reason. Along with raccoons, skunks often carry rabies. And if a terrier is sprayed by a skunk in close quarters (such as in a hole), the dog is at risk of dying. The spraying affects lung function and it is vital to immediately get the dog to a veterinarian to be put on oxygen and for other treatment. If the spraying is above ground, there are commercial products that are effective to reduce the odor. Also, bathing the dog in tomato juice is still accepted as being quite effective.

Porcupine quills must be removed quickly and completely by a veterinarian. The quills are very painful and will continue to imbed themselves deeper and deeper into the dog. There are cases where porcupine quills have caused the death of terriers. Treatment must not be delayed.

VOMITING

Vomiting should not be of any great concern if it does not persist. If your JR has eaten something that has upset his stomach, and he vomits, just keep a close eye on him. If he vomits three times or more and seems withdrawn or lethargic, call your veterinarian immediately, whether or not any other symptoms are present.

A FIRST-AID KIT

Keep a canine first-aid kit on hand for general care and emergencies. Check it periodically to make sure liquids haven't spilled or dried up, and replace medications and materials after they're used. Your kit should include:

Activated charcoal tablets

Adhesive tape
(1 and 2 inches wide)

Antibacterial ointment
(for skin and eyes)

Aspirin (buffered or enteric coated, *not* Ibuprofen)

Bandages: Gauze rolls (1 and 2 inches wide) and dressing pads

Cotton balls

Diarrhea medicine

Dosing syringe

Hydrogen peroxide (3%)

Petroleum jelly

Rectal thermometer

Rubber gloves

Rubbing alcohol

Scissors

Tourniquet

Towel

Tweezers

CHOKING

Choking can be a life-threatening condition. Puppies, curious by nature, are always picking up all sorts of objects, and are the most susceptible to choking on so many of the things that suit their fancy. You may be able to reach into the dog's throat and dislodge the object, or you may have to perform a Heimlich

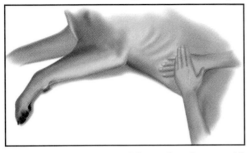

Applying abdominal thrusts can save a choking dog.

maneuver. (Lay the dog on his side and, with your palms just behind the last rib, give four quick thrusts. Check the mouth for the object and repeat the maneuver if necessary.) Some objects have been known to dislodge by holding the dog upside down. In a last-ditch effort to save his life, I had to perform a tracheotomy on one of my JRs in order to open an air passage. He had fallen unconscious and his heart had stopped beating. With that emergency action, mouth-to-muzzle resuscitation and gentle chest compression, the dog survived. He had been choking on a piece of rawhide.

POISONS

Poisons and toxins that can be dangerous for your Jack Russell are all over: house, garden, garage, everywhere. In your house may be such plants as dieffenbachia, philodendron, asparagus fern, ivy, poinsettia. Also dangerous are all the pesticides, cleaning supplies and medicines that must be closely guarded.

And then there is chocolate. Terriers love chocolate! A lethal dose consists of only one ounce of milk chocolate, or one-third ounce of dark chocolate, per pound of dog.

In the garden are acorns, lily of the valley, wisteria, daffodils, morning glory, holly, rhubarb and tomato vine, among others. And in the garage are any number of dangerous toxins, including the very common, sweet-tasting antifreeze (also a danger to children). Even a small amount carelessly left on the garage floor may kill.

If you suspect that your dog has been poisoned, immediate action is necessary. First, try to identify the poison, then call your veterinarian. If chemicals are involved, read the label and have it handy when you talk to your vet, or call a Poison Control Center for information on the chemical if the label is not informative. If your vet is not available, the Poison Control Center also can instruct you on the proper procedures to follow. Depending on the substance ingested, the length of time it has been in your dog's system and the dog's condition, you may be instructed to either induce vomiting with ipecac syrup or hydrogen peroxide, or give activated charcoal to delay or prevent absorption. Those items are important to have on hand, as well as other aids such as milk of magnesia and mineral oil.

Some of the many household substances harmful to your dog.

Symptoms of poisoning can range from obvious chocolate residue around your dog's mouth, to rashes on the skin or around the mouth, to vomiting and diarrhea, to hallucinations and convulsions, among others.

HEAT STROKE

Hyperthermia—heatstroke—occurs when the dog's internal temperature is higher than 104 degrees. (A dog's normal temperature is between 100 and 102 degrees.) Dogs cannot tolerate heat as well as humans. They must pant to cool their bodies and the only place they are able to sweat is through their foot pads. Heavy exertion, especially in hot weather, can be problematic. Since Jack Russells often do not know when to stop and rest to cool off, they may overdo it and show signs of hyperthermia. Symptoms include extreme weakness or panting, rapid breathing, vomiting and fainting. There may be an elevated heart rate.

In mild cases, moving the dog to an air-conditioned room may solve the problem. Apply cool compresses to the abdomen and groin and offer sips of cool water. For the more serious condition, cool the dog gradually in water. Do not try to bring down the temperature too rapidly. In all cases, call your veterinarian immediately. Serious hyperthermia can lead to coma and death.

Never, ever leave your dog in the car in warm weather—not even for a few minutes, even if the windows are opened for "ventilation." It is far better to leave the dog at home, no matter how much he loves to travel with you, if there is even a chance that you will have to leave him in the vehicle. Just a short stop at the store may put you at the end of a very long line at the checkout and temperatures in parked cars can reach life-threatening levels very, very quickly.

Run your hands regularly over your dog to feel for any injuries.

For the safety of your terrier, temperature extremes, hot or cold, are to be avoided. Be sure the dog has shade and other appropriate shelter when he is outdoors, as well as a good supply of fresh, cool water.

SHOCK

Shock is a danger to JRs who may have exerted themselves greatly and have been without water for a period of time. Shock may also result from accident, injury or blood loss. The dog will be weak and have pale gums, take shallow breaths and have a rapid, weak pulse. His eyes will have a glazed look and his body temperature will be low. Any dog in shock must be kept warm. Immediately wrap the dog in a blanket or your own jacket and get to a veterinarian as soon as possible.

DEHYDRATION

Dehydration is a danger in both hot and cold weather. Always remember to bring water with you for your terrier when hiking and enjoying other outdoor activities together.

BLEEDING

Bleeding requires that you remain calm if you are to help your dog. Try not to excite the dog, and talk to him to help him stay still. Apply gentle pressure on the wound with your hand or fingers, using a clean cloth if one is available. Dress the wound with a bandage, but do not pull it too tightly. You may apply an ice pack to keep the area cold in order to slow the bleeding. Get to a veterinarian, where the wound can be cleaned and sutured if necessary.

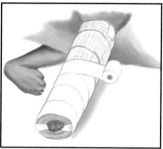

Make a temporary splint by wrapping the leg in firm casing, then bandaging it.

FRACTURES

Fractures may be indicated by the dog holding his injured leg off the ground or by cries of pain. If there is a fracture, you will need to get your terrier to the veterinarian immediately. The dog can be slipped onto a piece of plywood or other sturdy surface to be transported. Try to keep the injured limb from moving. It's good if someone can help you calm the dog and keep him immobile.

If there is no fracture, it is possible that the terrier picked up a thorn or other object that has punctured or become imbedded in the pad or the soft tissue between the toes.

LOSS OF APPETITE

If your terrier refuses to eat for more than a day or two, or has diarrhea or a cough, *call the veterinarian.* These could be symptoms of a number of ailments. (If the dog has diarrhea, remove all food but be sure fresh, clean water is available.)

*Use a scarf or
old hose to
make a tempo-
rary muzzle, as
shown.*

Jack Russells are tough little dogs and recover quickly from most any problem, but they do have a tendency to eat icky things, bringing on any number of consequences or, surprisingly, no consequences at all. My favorite true Jack-Russell-Terriers-eat-icky-things story happened one day when a neighbor's dog jumped up into a bush, caught a sparrow and consumed it in one giant swallow. His concerned owners called their veterinarian and asked what they should do. Knowing the breed well, the doctor mused for a moment and said, "May I suggest an orange sauce?"

Muzzles

Muzzles are important devices to learn about and have on hand. Even the sweetest dog in the world may try to bite you if you handle him when he is injured or in pain. Get a secure, comfortable muzzle and practice putting it on the dog for successively longer periods, up to a few minutes at a time. Try to make this fun, be gentle and reward him for calmly accepting the restraint. If your dog is at least familiar with a muzzle ahead of time, he may be spared the added anxiety of having to cope with a strange new device when he has been hurt.

If an emergency arises and you do not have a muzzle, you can make one from a strip of soft cloth, a necktie or even a stocking. Keep the dog calm and speak to him in a reassuring tone of voice. Holding one end of the cloth in each hand, make a loop and close it with a half knot. Slip the loop around the terrier's muzzle, with the half knot on top, and tighten it. Make a second loop around the muzzle and tighten it with a half knot underneath. Bring the ends of the cloth around the back of the neck and tie them together securely.

Giving Medication

PILLS

Giving a pill to a Jack Russell is easy. Just wrap it in cheese or insert it in a chunk of meat and it will be gone before you know it. If you can't do that, then open the dog's mouth, keep the head pointed upward and place the pill in the mouth as far back on the tongue as possible. Let the mouth close while still keeping the head looking up, massage the throat in a downward motion and gently blow toward the nostrils. This should make the dog swallow. No matter how the pill is administered, keep an eye on the dog to see if the pill hits the floor. Jack

To give a pill, open the mouth wide, then drop it in the back of the throat.

Russells are clever. You may need a few tries at getting the pill in your JR's mouth. The food-wrap method is much easier and almost always more successful.

LIQUID MEDICATION

If your veterinarian prescribes liquid medication for your Jack Russell Terrier, the easiest way to administer it is with a turkey baster or oral syringe. Tilt and hold the dog's head slightly back so the medicine runs into the mouth rather than out of it. Place the tip of the syringe in the back of the mouth between the molars and cheek, and squeeze the liquid out.

OINTMENT

To administer eye ointment, pull the lower lid slightly out and down to form a pocket. Squeeze a dab of ointment there and release the lid. As the dog blinks, the medication will be dispersed across the eye's surface.

To apply ointment to the skin, part the hair so that you are actually applying the medication to the affected area rather than to the surrounding hair.

85

In the case of a topical injury, your vet may prescribe an Elizabethan collar. This is a large, cone-shaped collar that will keep your JR from licking and scratching his wound and will allow it to heal more quickly. Your JR will not like it one bit, and will scratch at it and bother it, but try to make sure he keeps it on. Otherwise, the wound will take longer to heal and may become badly infected.

Taking Your JR's Temperature

One item you will want to keep in your first-aid kit is a rectal thermometer. In an emergency, your vet will

want to know as much about the situation as possible. Help with a quick diagnosis by having important first-aid devices on hand and knowing how to use them.

Hopefully, you will have someone to help you take your JR's temperature. Have your helper hold your dog's head and talk to him gently. Lift up the JR's tail and insert the well-lubricated thermometer into the anus about an inch. Hold on to it and don't let go. After three minutes, remove the thermometer, wipe it off and read the temperature. A dog's normal temperature is between 101 and 102 degrees.

An Elizabethan collar keeps your dog from licking a fresh wound.

Dog Fights

Dog fights are commonplace among Jack Russells. Not only will they fight among themselves, but they will often try to get it on with the biggest dog in the neighborhood, facing the danger that they will be shaken to death by a very annoyed animal many times their size.

Among themselves, same-sex fights are the most common, and fights between females have a history of being the most heated. It is not at all uncommon to have to place one of the offending scrappers in another household. Puncture wounds from dog fights have a tendency to become infected.

Prevention is the best cure. Keep your terrier contained in a securely fenced yard, or leashed when walking in public places. Keep no more than two JRs together, preferably spayed and neutered animals of the opposite sex.

Jack Russells don't seem to be put off by the size of the dog they are confronting.

If two dogs begin to square off, a distraction quickly created may end the episode. Throwing water on fighting dogs or sharply snapping a hound crop can sometimes end a confrontation if it has just begun. If the dogs are really into it and have a secure hold on each other, never try to pull them apart; you will cause more damage to the dogs and risk getting bitten yourself. In that situation, it is necessary to securely hold both dogs on the ground or floor until one lets go, at which time you have to move fast to get them locked away from each other permanently!

Once serious fighting has occurred between two particular dogs, it is likely that the animosity will continue and that they never will be able to be together again. Each one seems to hold a grudge against the other. Even a series of apparently minor scraps seem to escalate in seriousness with each successive altercation. Permanently separate the offending dogs at the beginning and avoid the possibility of serious injury or worse down the line. (There is a difference between the rough-and-tumble, seemingly angry play between two JRs and a real fight. You will clearly recognize that difference if you ever have the misfortune of being present when two JRs decide to take each other on.)

Spaying and Neutering

Neutering or spaying is the kindest thing you can do for your dog. And life with a dog is much easier for you, too, if you do not have to be concerned with the problems associated with the female's heat cycles or the male's compulsion to seek a female in season.

If a female is spayed at about six months of age, she is at virtually no risk of developing breast cancer. Because spaying involves removal of the uterus and ovaries, the danger of cancer in those organs is removed with them. Spaying also eliminates the mess associated with bleeding and the problems involved with having to isolate her for three to four weeks, twice a year, to keep her away from unneutered males. A bitch in season cannot be allowed out of your sight for even a moment. Keeping her in a kennel run or wire crate is no guarantee that a male will not get to her.

The female in heat has a strong desire to get to a male and her scent will attract unwanted males from far and wide. But this is just hormones and instinct at work. She has no innate "desire" to have babies. It is more than a misconception, it is simply untrue, that by

---

ADVANTAGES OF SPAY/NEUTER

The greatest advantage of spaying (for females) or neutering (for males) your dog is that you are guaranteed your dog will not produce puppies. There are too many puppies already available for too few homes. There are other advantages as well.

ADVANTAGES OF SPAYING

No messy heats.

No "suitors" howling at your windows or waiting in your yard.

Decreased incidences of pyometra (disease of the uterus) and breast cancer.

ADVANTAGES OF NEUTERING

Lessens male aggressive and territorial behaviors, but doesn't affect the dog's personality. Behaviors are often owner-induced, so neutering is not the only answer, but it is a good start.

Prevents the need to roam in search of bitches in season.

Decreased incidences of urogenital diseases.

allowing a bitch to have a litter she will be more "fulfilled" or become a better pet. A spayed bitch is more even in temperament than one who is cycling. And fights between female JRs often come up around the onset of heat cycles—a situation made worse by the fact that females living in the same household tend to cycle at about the same time.

Having an intact male in the house comes with its own set of problems, not the least of which is his tendency to mark his territory, inside the house as well as out. If he can detect a female in heat (his great sense of smell will let him know who is in season within a very large area) he will not only become a more prolific marker, he will become very restless and vocal in his cries. He may even lose his appetite. An intact male will go to great lengths to escape confinement, possibly harming himself in his efforts to locate the female.

Spayed and neutered animals will not become fat and lazy unless you let them. About the time when spaying and neutering can be done, the dog is nearing maturity and needing an adjustment in the type and amount of food being served. By keeping the diet appropriate to age and activity level, your dog will not get fat.

The only appropriate reason for keeping intact males or females is for breeding purposes, and animals kept for that purpose should, indeed, be especially fine examples of the breed, qualifying for registration with the JRTCA prior to breeding. They should be outstanding in quality, performance and temperament, free from any known genetic defects, and possess the working instincts that have kept this dog what it is for so many years.

Far too many people these days seem to think that having a litter of puppies might be an easy way to make some money. Serious breeders have plans and goals for their breeding programs. They study the art of breeding and have a deep moral and financial commitment to their dogs and the puppies they allow to come into the world. There is simply no quick and easy way to harvest puppies for sale at a profit, while still

Living with a
Jack Russell
Terrier

maintaining the ethical standards required of an honest, dedicated breeder. Most serious breeders spend more than they make, or just barely break even, because their motivation is based on love of their dogs, and their long-term goal is the improvement of the breed.

Jack Russells love their people and look to them for affection and guidance. A JR with a loving owner who has time to play, time for exercise and time for making him a part of family life is a dog that is truly "fulfilled." He will have a happy, meaningful life without reproduction being a part of it. The burden of unwanted pets needing homes is enormous, and frivolous breeding adds greatly to the problem—especially with a complicated little dog like the Jack Russell Terrier.

Problems Particular to the Jack Russell

Some genetic problems have been found in Jack Russells but, fortunately, fewer than are found in some other breeds. Perhaps that is a result of less inbreeding. Dogs with known defects should not be bred.

Patella luxation is the equivalent of a slipped kneecap in humans. When the kneecap (patella) becomes dislocated, there may be pain and difficulty straightening the knee. The luxation may be permanent or it may be intermittent, with the kneecap popping in and out of position. The dog may move in a normal manner one minute and be lame the next.

This condition can lead to the premature development of arthritis and restricted, painful movement. This is the last thing one wants an eager, active dog like the Jack Russell to go through. If the condition becomes painful, corrective surgery is the preferred treatment, and patients usually recover fully.

Legg-Perthes disease is seen in small dogs and is similar to a condition that affects children. It is caused by destruction of the ball-and-socket hip joint. Permanent arthritis may be a result of Legg-Perthes.

Deafness shows up often in white-coated animals. The dog may be totally deaf (bilateral) or deaf in only one ear (unilateral). Unilateral deafness is more difficult to detect as the dog quickly learns to compensate for his loss in the one deaf ear. A BAER (brain-stem auditory evoked response) test is used to detect deafness. Electrodes are placed on the dog's head and the path is transmitted through the brain to a receiver. A pattern is recorded showing whether or not the brain is responding to the transmissions.

It takes a very dedicated owner with very special abilities to provide for the protection and safety of a totally deaf Jack Russell. Some have fared well living with hearing dogs, or with deaf people who have taught the dog sign language. But there are also incidents of biting which have occurred as a result of an exaggerated startle response from a profoundly deaf dog. Some feel that humane euthanasia is the best choice for these dogs. A unilaterally deaf dog makes a wonderful pet, but it must not be bred. It is strongly suggested that all breeding stock be BAER tested before they are bred. The test is not difficult or painful for the dog.

A hernia is a protrusion of an organ or tissue through a body wall. In JRs, there are umbilical and inguinal hernias. A dog born with a hernia should not be bred.

Lens luxation, a dislocation of the lens, usually appears during a dog's middle age. It is an inherited disease of the tissues that hold the lens

IDENTIFYING YOUR DOG

It's a terrible thing to think about, but your dog could somehow, someday, get lost or stolen. How would you get him back? Your best bet would be to have some form of identification on your dog. You can choose from a collar and tags, a tattoo, a microchip or a combination of these three.

Every dog should wear a buckle collar with identification tags. They are the quickest and easiest way for a stranger to identify your dog. It's best to inscribe the tags with your name and phone number; you don't need to include your dog's name.

There are two ways to permanently identify your dog. The first is a tattoo, placed on the inside of your dog's thigh. The tattoo should be your social security number or your dog's JRTCA registration number.

The second is a microchip, a rice-sized pellet that's inserted under the dog's skin at the base of the neck, between the shoulder blades. When a scanner is passed over the dog, it will beep, notifying the person that the dog has a chip. The scanner will then show a code, identifying the dog. Microchips are becoming more and more popular and are certainly the wave of the future.

in place. Both eyes are usually affected and secondary glaucoma may result.

Surgery will remove the affected lens or lenses. Vision after surgery will be reduced but still present, whereas glaucoma will gradually destroy vision altogether. This treatment, while not perfect, is certainly preferable to ensuing blindness.

High toes have been seen on Jack Russells. This involves a toe that is set high on the foot, usually on the outside. It occurs mainly on the front feet but has been found on back feet also. This defect may appear in some bloodlines and is being studied.

von Willibrand's Disease (vWD) is the most common inherited bleeding disorder in dogs. This is not hemophilia, in which only males are affected by the disorder passed on from their mothers. Von Willibrand's Disease is carried by both males and females, and both males and females can be affected.

Bleeding in affected individuals is caused by deficiency or dysfunction of the von Willibrand factor (vWF) protein, normally found in plasma and critical in the control of bleeding. A dog may be a carrier but not be affected and not show any symptoms. Affected dogs may show such symptoms as spontaneous bleeding from mucous membrane linings of the nose or mouth, or prolonged bleeding from sites of trauma or surgery, or even after clipping a nail too short.

In addition to having been found in over fifty breeds of dogs, vWD has been seen in mixed breed dogs, cats, horses, pigs and human beings. It is not common in Jack Russells, but it has been found. There is no continuous treatment for vWD, though a drug can be administered to increase clotting when necessary. As it is known to be hereditary, any dog with a history of this disease in his background should be tested. Dogs can be tested for it prior to breeding.

Old Age and Euthanasia

The Jack Russell retains his energy and wild instincts throughout his life. Though he may settle down a bit as he gets older, nap more, eat more, never for a moment believe that he has retired or abandoned the craziness of his younger years.

Jack Russells have amazing healing potential and are extremely tough. There are remarkable stories about JRs struggling back from near-death experiences. In one extraordinary case, a Jack Russell died and was actually buried by his sad owner. When the dog reappeared at the door, the family was amazed and the story reached the news!

Your older JR may nap more, but never believe she has abandoned her youthful ways.

Few Jack Russells die of old age. In fact, according to Alisa Crawford, founder and first registrar of the Jack Russell Terrier Club of America, cars are the number one killer of these little dogs. Some JRs self-destruct with their tendencies toward mishap and mischief; in constant motion, they do not even notice their own endings. On the other hand, some do seem to know and communicate a warning or farewell to a sensitive owner.

Nigel, a fourteen-year-old Jack Russell, passed away with the new year. He had vanished from his farm home for three days while the weather was harsh and winds and rains made the nights more dreadful. The farm is near two busy roads and his owners were frantic. They could not find him anywhere, and he returned around Christmas exhausted and injured. He spent Christmas with his family, but only a few days later they heard him whining as he lay curled up in their bed. By the time they turned on the light, he was gone.

My own favorite old dog was Nester Acorn, who was responsible for launching me into dogdom. One day, while I was walking my terriers, Nester cut from the pack and made a beeline to his favorite hole on the steep edge of a gully not far from our house. This hole had housed foxes for years and was a powerful magnet to Nester. His eagerness to get to that spot was a good example of the kind of compulsive JRT behavior that has been discussed elsewhere in this book.

Nester vanished deep into the earth and expired somewhere far below. This is certainly the way he would have chosen to go, as he was the essence of the working terrier. Many JRTs die in the line of duty, due to the compulsion of their prey-focused behavior. It is their instinct, their nature and sometimes their final calling.

Those of us bound by a deep level of partnership and friendship to a JR will mourn his passing greatly. Other terrier owners will best understand the profound loss of your canine friend. Every person will grieve differently, but it may take a long time to overcome the sadness occasioned by the loss of a beloved canine pal.

Some animals need to be put to sleep to be released from suffering. If the dog stands little chance of recovery and his suffering is painful and intense, euthanasia may be the only humane choice. Be sensitive to the situation and feelings of your dog, and you will know the right thing to do. Understanding the message of a beloved terrier is possible, and many are able to communicate their will to their owners.

Your Happy, Healthy Pet

Your Dog's Name _____

Name on Your Dog's Pedigree (if your dog has one) _____

_____

Where Your Dog Came From _____

_____

Your Dog's Birthday _____

Your Dog's Veterinarian

    Name _____

    Address _____

    Phone Number _____

    Emergency Number _____

Your Dog's Health

    Vaccines

    type _____ date given _____

    type _____ date given _____

    type _____ date given _____

    type _____ date given _____

    Heartworm

    date tested _____ type used_____ start date _____

Your Dog's License Number _____

Groomer's Name and Number _____

Dogsitter/Walker's Name and Number _____

Awards Your Dog Has Won

    Award _____ date earned _____

    Award _____ date earned _____

part three

Enjoying your Dog

chapter 8

Basic
Training

by Ian Dunbar, Ph.D., MRCVS

Training is the jewel in the crown—the most important aspect of doggy husbandry. There is no more important variable influencing dog behavior and temperament than the dog's education: A well-trained, well-behaved and good-natured puppydog is always a joy to live with, but an untrained and uncivilized dog can be a perpetual nightmare. Moreover, deny the dog an education and it will not have the opportunity to fulfill its own canine potential; neither will it have the ability to communicate effectively with its human companions.

Luckily, modern psychological training methods are easy, efficient and effective and, above all, considerably dog-friendly and user-friendly. Doggy education is as simple as it is enjoyable. But before you can have a good time play-training with your new dog, you have to learn what to do and how to do it. There is no bigger variable influencing the success of dog training than the *owner's* experience and expertise. *Before you embark on the dog's education, you must first educate yourself.*

Basic Training for Owners

Ideally, basic owner training should begin well *before* you select your dog. Find out all you can about your chosen breed first, then master rudimentary training and handling skills. If you already have your puppy/dog, owner training is a dire emergency—the clock is running! Especially for puppies, the first few weeks at home are the most important and influential days in the dog's life. Indeed, the cause of most adolescent and adult problems may be traced back to the initial days the pup explores his new home. This is the time to establish the *status quo*—to teach the puppy/dog how you would like him to behave and so prevent otherwise quite predictable problems.

In addition to consulting breeders and breed books such as this one (which understandably have a positive breed bias), seek out as many pet owners with your breed you can find. Good points are obvious. What you want to find out are the breed-specific *problems*, so you can nip them in the bud. In particular, you should talk to owners with *adolescent* dogs and make a list of all anticipated problems. Most important, *test drive* at least half a dozen adolescent and adult dogs of your breed yourself. An eight-week-old puppy is deceptively easy to handle, but she will acquire adult size, speed and strength in just four months, so you should learn now what to prepare for.

Puppy and pet dog training classes offer a convenient venue to locate pet owners and observe dogs in action. For a list of suitable trainers in your area, contact the Association of Pet Dog Trainers (see Chapter 13). You may also begin your basic owner training by observing other owners in class. Watch as many classes and test drive as many dogs as possible. Select an upbeat, dog-friendly, people-friendly, fun-and-games, puppydog pet training class to learn the ropes. Also, watch training videos and read training books (see Chapter 12). You must find out what to do and how to do it *before* you have to do it.

Principles of Training

Most people think training comprises teaching the dog to do things such as sit, speak and roll over, but even a four-week-old pup knows how to do these things already. Instead, the first step in training involves teaching the dog human words for each dog behavior and activity and for each aspect of the dog's environment. That way you, the owner, can more easily participate in the dog's domestic education by directing him to perform specific actions appropriately, that is, at the right time, in the right place, and so on. Training opens communication channels, enabling an educated dog to at least understand the owner's requests.

In addition to teaching a dog *what* we want her to do, it is also necessary to teach her *why* she should do what we ask. Indeed, 95 percent of training revolves around motivating the dog *to want to do* what we want. Dogs often understand what their owners want; they just don't see the point of doing it—especially when the owner's repetitively boring and seemingly senseless instructions are totally at odds with much more pressing and exciting doggy distractions. It is not so much the dog who is being stubborn or dominant; rather, it is the owner who has failed to acknowledge the dog's needs and feelings and to approach training from the dog's point of view.

The Meaning of Instructions

The secret to successful training is learning how to use training lures to predict or prompt specific behaviors—to coax the dog to do what you want *when* you want. Any highly valued object (such as a treat or toy) may be used as a lure, which the dog will follow with his eyes and nose. Moving the lure in specific ways entices the dog to move his nose, head and entire body in specific ways. In fact, by learning the art of manipulating various lures, it is possible to teach the dog to assume virtually any body position and perform any action. Once you have control over the expression of the dog's behaviors and can elicit any body position or behavior at will, you can easily teach the dog to perform on request.

Tell your dog what you want him to do, use a lure to entice him to respond correctly, then profusely praise

Teach your dog words for each activity he needs to know, like down.

and maybe reward him once he performs the desired action. For example, verbally request "Fido, sit!" while you move a squeaky toy upwards and backwards over the dog's muzzle (lure-movement and hand signal), smile knowingly as he looks up (to follow the lure) and sits down (as a result of canine anatomical engineering), then praise him to distraction ("Gooood Fido!"). Squeak the toy, offer a training treat and give your dog and yourself a pat on the back.

Being able to elicit desired responses over and over enables the owner to reward the dog over and over. Consequently, the dog begins to think training is fun. For example, the more the dog is rewarded for sitting, the more she enjoys sitting. Eventually the dog comes to realize that, whereas most sitting is appreciated, sitting immediately upon request usually prompts especially enthusiastic praise and a slew of high-level rewards. The dog begins to sit on cue much of the time, showing that she is starting to grasp the meaning of the owner's verbal request and hand signal.

Why Comply?

Most dogs enjoy initial lure/reward training and are only too happy to comply with their owners' wishes. Unfortunately, repetitive drilling without appreciative feedback tends to diminish the dog's enthusiasm until he eventually fails to see the point of complying anymore. Moreover, as the dog approaches adolescence he becomes more easily distracted as he develops other interests. Lengthy sessions with repetitive exercises tend to bore and demotivate both parties. If it's not fun, the owner doesn't do it and neither does the dog.

Integrate training into your dog's life: The greater number of training sessions each day and the *shorter* they are, the more willingly compliant your dog will become. Make sure to have a short (just a few seconds) training interlude before every enjoyable canine activity. For example, ask your dog to sit to greet people, to sit before you throw his Frisbee, and to sit for his supper. Really, sitting is no different from a canine "please." Also, include numerous short training interludes during every enjoyable canine pastime, for example, when playing with the dog or when he is running in the park. In this fashion, doggy distractions may be effectively converted into rewards for training. Just as all games have rules, fun becomes training . . . and training becomes fun.

Eventually, rewards actually become unnecessary to continue motivating your dog. If trained with consideration and kindness, performing the desired behaviors will become self-rewarding and, in a sense, your dog will motivate himself. Just as it is not necessary to reward a human companion during an enjoyable walk in the park, or following a game of tennis, it is hardly necessary to reward our best friend—the dog—for walking by our side or while playing fetch. Human company during enjoyable activities is reward enough for most dogs.

Even though your dog has become self-motivating, it's still good to praise and pet him a lot and offer rewards once in a while, especially for a good job well done. And if for no other reason, praising and rewarding others is good for the human heart.

To train your dog, you need gentle hands, a loving heart and a good attitude.

Punishment

Without a doubt, lure/reward training is by far the best way to teach: Entice your dog to do what you want and then reward him for doing so. Unfortunately, a human shortcoming is to take the good for granted and to moan and groan at the bad. Specifically, the dog's many good behaviors are ignored while the owner focuses on punishing the dog for making mistakes. In extreme cases, instruction is *limited* to punishing mistakes made by a trainee dog, child, employee or husband, even though it has been proven punishment training is notoriously inefficient and ineffective and is decidedly unfriendly and combative. It teaches the dog that training is a drag, almost as quickly as it teaches the dog to dislike his trainer. Why treat our best friends like our worst enemies?

Punishment training is also much more laborious and time consuming. Whereas it takes only a finite amount of time to teach a dog what to chew, for example, it takes much, much longer to punish the dog for each and every mistake. Remember, *there is only one right way!* So why not teach that right way from the outset?!

To make matters worse, punishment training causes severe lapses in the dog's reliability. Since it is obviously impossible to punish the dog each and every time she misbehaves, the dog quickly learns to distinguish between those times when she must comply (so as to avoid impending punishment) and those times when she need not comply, because punishment is impossible. Such times include when the dog is off leash and only six feet away, when the owner is otherwise engaged (talking to a friend, watching television, taking a shower, tending to the baby or chatting on the telephone), or when the dog is left at home alone.

Instances of misbehavior will be numerous when the owner is away, because even when the dog complied in the owner's looming presence, he did so unwillingly. The dog was forced to act against his will, rather than moulding his will to want to please. Hence, when the owner is absent, not only does the dog know he need not comply, he simply does not want to. Again, the trainee is not a stubborn vindictive beast, but rather the trainer has failed to teach.

Punishment training invariably creates unpredictable Jekyll and Hyde behavior.

Trainer's Tools

Many training books extol the virtues of a vast array of training paraphernalia and electronic and metallic gizmos, most of which are designed for canine restraint, correction and punishment, rather than for actual facilitation of doggy education. In reality, most effective training tools are not found in stores; they come from within ourselves. In addition to a willing dog, all you really need is a functional human brain, gentle hands, a loving heart and a good attitude.

In terms of equipment, all dogs do require a quality buckle collar to sport dog tags and to attach the leash (for safety and to comply with local leash laws). Hollow chewtoys (like Kongs or sterilized longbones) and a dog bed or collapsible crate are a must for housetraining. Three additional tools are required:

1. specific lures (training treats and toys) to predict and prompt specific desired behaviors;

2. rewards (praise, affection, training treats and toys) to reinforce for the dog what a lot of fun it all is; and

3. knowledge—how to convert the dog's favorite activities and games (potential distractions to training) into "life-rewards," which may be employed to facilitate training.

The most powerful of these is *knowledge*. Education is the key! Watch training classes, participate in training classes, watch videos, read books, enjoy playtraining with your dog, and then your dog will say "Please," and your dog will say "Thank you!"

Housetraining

If dogs were left to their own devices, certainly they would chew, dig and bark for entertainment and then no doubt highlight a few areas of their living space with sprinkles of urine, in much the same way we decorate by hanging pictures. Consequently, when we ask a dog to live with us, we must teach him *where* he may dig and perform his toilet duties, *what* he may chew and *when* he may bark. After all, when left at home alone for many hours, we cannot expect the dog to amuse himself by completing crosswords or watching the soaps on TV!

Also, it would be decidedly unfair to keep the house rules a secret from the dog, and then get angry and punish the poor critter for inevitably transgressing rules he did not even know existed. Remember, without adequate education and guidance, the dog will be forced to establish his own rules—doggy rules—that most probably will be at odds with the owner's view of domestic living.

Since most problems develop during the first few days the dog is at home, prospective dog owners must be certain they are quite clear about the principles of housetraining *before* they get a dog. Early misbehaviors quickly become established as the status quo—

Enjoying Your
Dog

becoming firmly entrenched as hard-to-break bad habits, which set the precedent for years to come. Make sure to teach your dog good habits right from the start. Good habits are just as hard to break as bad ones!

Ideally, when a new dog comes home, try to arrange for someone to be present for as much as possible during the first few days (for adult dogs) or weeks for puppies. With only a little forethought, it is surprisingly easy to find a puppy sitter, such as a retired person, who would be willing to eat from your refrigerator and watch your television while keeping an eye on the newcomer to encourage the dog to play with chewtoys and to ensure he goes outside on a regular basis.

POTTY TRAINING

To teach the dog where to relieve himself:

1. never let him make a single mistake;
2. let him know where you want him to go; and
3. handsomely reward him for doing so: "GOOOOOOOD DOG!!!" liver treat, liver treat, liver treat!

PREVENTING MISTAKES

A single mistake is a training disaster, since it heralds many more in future weeks. And each time the dog soils the house, this further reinforces the dog's unfortunate preference for an indoor, carpeted toilet. *Do not let an unhousetrained dog have full run of the house if you are away from home or cannot pay full attention.* Instead, confine the dog to an area where elimination is appropriate, such as an outdoor run or, better still, a small, comfortable indoor kennel with access to an outdoor run. When confined in this manner, most dogs will naturally housetrain themselves.

If that's not possible, confine the dog to an area, such as a utility room, kitchen, basement or garage, where elimination may not be desired in the long run but as an interim measure it is certainly preferable to doing it all around the house. Use newspaper to cover the floor of the dog's day room. The newspaper may be used to soak up the urine and to wrap up and dispose of the feces. Once your dog develops a preferred spot for eliminating, it is only necessary to cover that part of the floor with newspaper. The smaller papered area may then be moved (only a little each day) towards the door to the outside. Thus the dog will develop the tendency to go to the door when he needs to relieve himself.

Never confine an unhousetrained dog to a crate for long periods. Doing so would force the dog to soil the crate and ruin its usefulness as an aid for housetraining (see the following discussion).

The first few weeks at home are the most important and influential in your dog's life.

TEACHING WHERE

In order to teach your dog where you would like her to do her business, you have to be there to direct the proceedings—an obvious, yet often neglected, fact of life. In order to be there to teach the dog *where* to go, you need to know *when* she needs to go. Indeed, the success of housetraining depends on the owner's ability to predict these times. Certainly, a regular feeding schedule will facilitate prediction somewhat, but there is

nothing like "loading the deck" and influencing the timing of the outcome yourself!

Whenever you are at home, make sure the dog is under constant supervision and/or confined to a small

area. If already well trained, simply instruct the dog to
lie down in his bed or basket. Alternatively, confine the
dog to a crate (doggy den) or tie-down (a short, 18-
inch lead that can be clipped to an eye hook in the
baseboard). Short-term close confinement strongly
inhibits urination and defecation, since the dog does
not want to soil his sleeping area. Thus, when you
release the puppydog each hour, he will definitely
need to urinate immediately and defecate every third
or fourth hour. Keep the dog confined to his doggy
den and take him to his intended toilet area each hour,
every hour, and on the hour.

When taking your dog outside, instruct him to sit qui-
etly before opening the door—he will soon learn to sit
by the door when he needs to go out!

TEACHING WHY

Being able to predict when the dog needs to go
enables the owner to be on the spot to praise and
reward the dog. Each hour, hurry the dog to the
intended toilet area in the yard, issue the appropriate
instruction ("Go pee!" or "Go poop!"), then give the
dog three to four minutes to produce. Praise and offer
a couple of training treats when successful. The treats
are important because many people fail to praise their
dogs with feeling . . . and housetraining is hardly the
time for understatement. So either loosen up and
enthusiastically praise that dog: "Wuzzzer-wuzzer-
wuzzer, hoooser good wuffer den? Hoooo went pee for
Daddy?" Or say "Good dog!" as best you can and offer
the treats for effect.

Following elimination is an ideal time for a spot of
playtraining in the yard or house. Also, an empty dog
may be allowed greater freedom around the house for
the next half hour or so, just as long as you keep an eye
out to make sure he does not get into other kinds of
mischief. If you are preoccupied and cannot pay full
attention, confine the dog to his doggy den once more
to enjoy a peaceful snooze or to play with his many
chewtoys.

If your dog does not eliminate within the allotted time outside—no biggie! Back to his doggy den, and then try again after another hour.

As I own large dogs, I always feel more relaxed walking an empty dog, knowing that I will not need to finish our stroll weighted down with bags of feces! Beware of falling into the trap of walking the dog to get it to eliminate. The good ol' dog walk is such an enormous highlight in the dog's life that it represents the single biggest potential reward in domestic dogdom. However, when in a hurry, or during inclement weather, many owners abruptly terminate the walk the moment the dog has done its business. This, in effect, severely punishes the dog for doing the right thing, in the right place at the right time. Consequently, many dogs become strongly inhibited from eliminating outdoors because they know it will signal an abrupt end to an otherwise thoroughly enjoyable walk.

Instead, instruct the dog to relieve himself in the yard prior to going for a walk. If you follow the above instructions, most dogs soon learn to eliminate on cue. As soon as the dog eliminates, praise (and offer a treat or two)—"Good dog! Let's go walkies!" Use the walk as a reward for eliminating in the yard. If the dog does not go, put him back in his doggy den and think about a walk later on. You will find with a "No feces–no walk" policy, your dog will become one of the fastest defecators in the business.

If you do not have a back yard, instruct the dog to eliminate right outside your front door prior to the walk. Not only will this facilitate clean up and disposal of the feces in your own trash can but, also, the walk may again be used as a colossal reward.

CHEWING AND BARKING

Short-term close confinement also teaches the dog that occasional quiet moments are a reality of domestic living. Your puppydog is extremely impressionable during his first few weeks at home. Regular confinement at this time soon exerts a calming influence over the dog's personality. Remember, once the dog is housetrained and calmer, there will be a whole lifetime ahead for the dog to enjoy full run of the house and garden. On the other hand, by letting the newcomer have unrestricted access to the entire household and allowing him to run willy-nilly, he will most certainly develop a bunch of behavior problems in short order, no doubt necessitating confinement later in life. It would not be fair to remedially restrain and confine a dog you have trained, through neglect, to run free.

When confining the dog, make sure he always has an impressive array of suitable chewtoys. Kongs and sterilized longbones (both readily available from pet stores) make the best chewtoys, since they are hollow and may be stuffed with treats to heighten the dog's interest. For example, by stuffing the little hole at the top of a Kong with a small piece of freeze-dried liver, the dog will not want to leave it alone.

Remember, treats do not have to be junk food and they certainly should not represent extra calories. Rather, treats should be part of each dog's regular daily diet:

Make sure your puppy has suit able chewtoys.

Some food may be served in the dog's bowl for breakfast and dinner, some food may be used as training treats, and some food may be used for stuffing chewtoys. I regularly stuff my dogs' many Kongs with different shaped biscuits and kibble. The kibble seems to fall out fairly easily, as do the oval-shaped biscuits, thus rewarding the dog instantaneously for checking out the chewtoys. The bone-shaped biscuits fall out after a while, rewarding the dog for worrying at the chewtoy. But the triangular biscuits never come out. They remain inside the Kong as lures, maintaining the dog's fascination with its chewtoy. To further focus the dog's interest, I always make sure to flavor the triangular biscuits by rubbing them with a little cheese or freeze-dried liver.

If stuffed chewtoys are reserved especially for times the dog is confined, the puppydog will soon learn to enjoy quiet moments in her doggy den and she will quickly develop a chewtoy habit—a good habit! This is a simple *passive training* process; all the owner has to do is set up the situation and the dog all but trains herself—easy and effective. Even when the dog is given run of the house, her first inclination will be to indulge her rewarding chewtoy habit rather than destroying less-attractive household articles, such as curtains, carpets, chairs and compact disks. Similarly, a chewtoy chewer will be less inclined to scratch and chew herself excessively. Also, if the dog busies herself as a recreational chewer, she will be less inclined to develop into a recreational barker or digger when left at home alone.

Stuff a number of chewtoys whenever the dog is left confined and remove the extra-special-tasting treats when you return. Your dog will now amuse himself with his chewtoys before falling asleep and then resume playing with his chewtoys when he expects you to return. Since most owner-absent misbehavior happens right after you leave and right before your expected return, your puppydog will now be conveniently preoccupied with his chewtoys at these times.

To teach come, call your dog, open your arms as a welcoming signal, wave a toy or a treat and praise for every step in your direction.

Come and Sit

Most puppies will happily approach virtually anyone, whether called or not; that is, until they collide with adolescence and develop other more important doggy interests, such as sniffing a multiplicity of exquisite odors on the grass. Your mission, Mr. and/or Ms. Owner, is to teach and reward the pup for coming reliably, willingly and happily when called—and you have just three months to get it done. Unless adequately reinforced, your puppy's tendency to approach people will self-destruct by adolescence.

Call your dog ("Fido, come!"), open your arms (and maybe squat down) as a welcoming signal, waggle a treat or toy as a lure, and reward the puppydog when he comes running. Do not wait to praise the dog until he reaches you—he may come 95 percent of the way and then run off after some distraction. Instead, praise the dog's *first* step towards you and continue praising enthusiastically for *every* step he takes in your direction.

When the rapidly approaching puppy dog is three lengths away from impact, instruct him to sit ("Fido, sit!") and hold the lure in front of you in an outstretched hand to prevent him from hitting you mid-chest and knocking you flat on your back! As Fido decelerates to nose the lure, move the treat upwards and backwards just over his muzzle with an upwards motion of your extended arm (palm-upwards). As the dog looks up to follow the lure, he will sit down (if he jumps up, you are holding the lure too high). Praise the dog for sitting. Move backwards and call him again. Repeat this many times over, always praising when Fido comes and sits; on occasion, reward him.

For the first couple of trials, use a training treat both as a lure to entice the dog to come and sit and as a reward for doing so. Thereafter, try to use different items as lures and rewards. For example, lure the dog with a Kong or Frisbee but reward her with a food treat. Or lure the dog with a food treat but pat her and throw a tennis ball as a reward. After just a few repetitions, dispense with the lures and rewards; the dog will begin to respond willingly to your verbal requests and hand signals just for the prospect of praise from your heart and affection from your hands.

Instruct every family member, friend and visitor how to get the dog to come and sit. Invite people over for a series of pooch parties; do not keep the pup a secret— let other people enjoy this puppy, and let the pup enjoy other people. Puppydog parties are not only fun, they easily attract a lot of people to help *you* train *your* dog. Unless you teach your dog *how* to meet people, that is, to sit for greetings, no doubt the dog will resort to jumping up. Then you and the visitors will get annoyed, and the dog will be punished. This is not fair. *Send out those invitations for puppy parties and teach your dog to be mannerly and socially acceptable.*

Even though your dog quickly masters obedient recalls in the house, his reliability may falter when playing in the back yard or local park. Ironically, it is *the owner* who has unintentionally trained the dog *not* to respond in these instances. By allowing the dog to play and run around and otherwise have a good time, but then to call the dog to put him on leash to take him home, the dog quickly learns playing is fun but training is a drag. Thus, playing in the park becomes a severe distraction, which works against training. Bad news!

Instead, whether playing with the dog off leash or on leash, request him to come at frequent intervals— say, every minute or so. On most occasions, praise and pet the dog for a few seconds while he is sitting, then tell him to go play again. For especially fast recalls, offer a couple of training treats and take the time to praise and pet the dog enthusiastically before releasing him. The dog will learn that coming when called is not necessarily the end of the play session, and neither is it the end of the world; rather, it signals an enjoyable, quality time-out with the owner before resuming play once more. In fact, playing in the park now becomes a very effective life-reward, which works to facilitate training by reinforcing each obedient and timely recall. Good news!

Sit, Down, Stand and Rollover

Teaching the dog a variety of body positions is easy for owner and dog, impressive for spectators and extremely useful for all. Using lure-reward techniques, it is possible to train several positions at once to verbal commands or hand signals (which impress the socks off onlookers).

Sit and *down*—the two control commands—prevent or resolve nearly a hundred behavior problems. For example, if the dog happily and obediently sits or lies down when requested, he cannot jump on visitors, dash out the front door, run around and chase its tail, pester other dogs, harass cats or annoy family, friends or strangers. Additionally, "sit" or "down" are better emergency commands for off-leash control.

It is easier to teach and maintain a reliable sit than maintain a reliable recall. *Sit* is the purest and simplest of commands—either the dog is sitting or he is not. If there is any change of circumstances or potential danger in the park, for example, simply instruct the dog to sit. If he sits, you have a number of options: allow the dog to resume playing when he is safe; walk up and put the dog on leash, or call the dog. The dog will be much more likely to come when called if he has already acknowledged his compliance by sitting. If the dog does not sit in the park—train him to!

Stand and *rollover-stay* are the two positions for examining the dog. Your veterinarian will love you to distraction if you take a little time to teach the dog to stand still and roll over and play possum. Also, your vet bills will be smaller. The rollover-stay is an especially useful command and is really just a variation of the down-stay: whereas the dog lies prone in the traditional down, she lies supine in the rollover-stay.

As with teaching come and sit, the training techniques to teach the dog to assume all other body positions on cue are user-friendly and dog-friendly. Simply give the appropriate request, lure the dog into the desired body position using a training treat or toy and then *praise* (and maybe reward) the dog as soon as he complies. Try not to touch the dog to get him to respond. If you teach the dog by guiding him into position, the dog will quickly learn that rump-pressure means sit, for example, but as yet you still have no control over your dog if he is just six feet away. It will still be necessary to teach the dog to sit on request. So do not make training a time-consuming two-step process; instead, teach the dog to sit to a verbal request or hand signal from the outset. Once the dog sits willingly when requested, by all means use your hands to pet the dog when he does so.

To teach *down* when the dog is already sitting, say "Fido, down!," hold the lure in one hand (palm down) and lower that hand to the floor between the dog's forepaws. As the dog lowers his head to follow the lure, slowly move the lure away from the dog just a fraction (in front of his paws). The dog will lie down as he stretches his nose forward to follow the lure. Praise the dog when he does so. If the dog stands up, you pulled the lure away too far and too quickly.

When teaching the dog to lie down from the standing position, say "down" and lower the lure to the floor as before. Once the dog has lowered his forequarters and assumed a play bow, gently and slowly move the lure *towards* the dog between his forelegs. Praise the dog as soon as his rear end plops down.

After just a couple of trials it will be possible to alternate sits and downs and have the dog energetically perform doggy push-ups. Praise the dog a lot, and after half a dozen or so push-ups reward the dog with a training treat or toy. You will notice the more energetically you move your arm—upwards (palm up) to get the dog to sit, and downwards (palm down) to get the dog to lie down—the more energetically the dog responds to your requests. Now try training the dog in silence and you will notice he has also learned to respond to hand signals. Yeah! Not too shabby for the first session.

To teach *stand* from the sitting position, say "Fido, stand," slowly move the lure half a dog-length away from the dog's nose, keeping it at nose level, and praise the dog as he stands to follow the lure. As soon

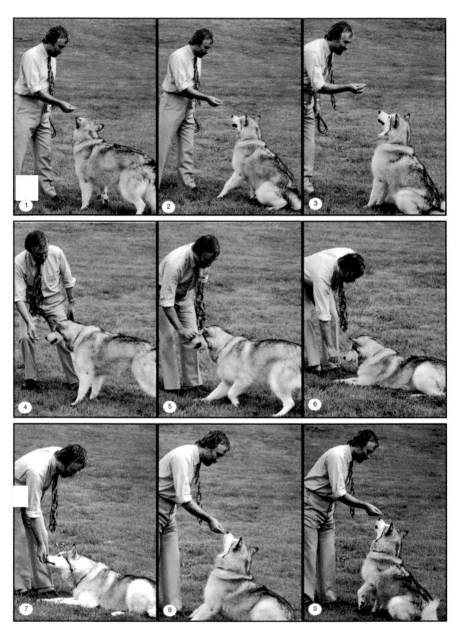

Using a food lure to teach sit, down and stand. 1) "Phoenix, Sit." 2) Hand palm upwards, move lure up and back over dog's muzzle. 3) "Good sit, Phoenix!" 4) "Phoenix, down." 5) Hand palm downwards, move lure down to lie between dog's forepaws. 6) "Phoenix, off. Good down, Phoenix!" 7) "Phoenix, sit!" 8) Palm upwards, move lure up and back, keeping it close to dog's muzzle. 9) "Good sit, Phoenix!"

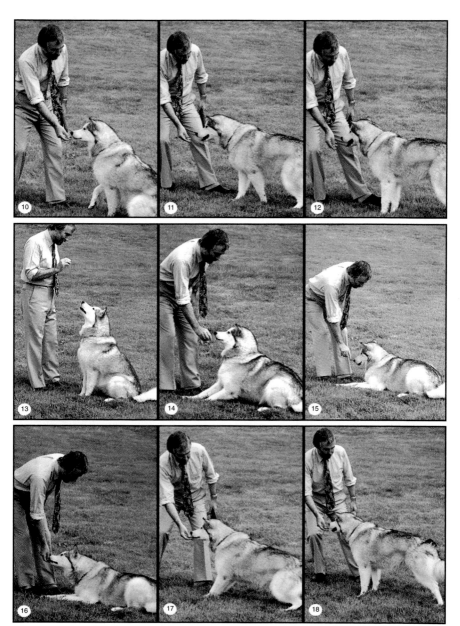

10) *"Phoenix, stand!"* 11) *Move lure away from dog at nose height, then lower it a tad.* 12) *"Phoenix, off! Good stand, Phoenix!"* 13) *"Phoenix, down!"* 14) *Hand palm downwards, move lure down to lie between dog's forepaws.* 15) *"Phoenix, off! Good down-stay, Phoenix!"* 16) *"Phoenix, stand!"* 17) *Move lure away from dog's muzzle up to nose height.* 18) *"Phoenix,off! Good stand-stay, Phoenix. Now we'll make the vet and groomer happy!"*

as the dog stands, lower the lure to just beneath the dog's chin to entice him to look down; otherwise he will stand and then sit immediately. To prompt the dog to stand from the down position, move the lure half a dog-length upwards and away from the dog, holding the lure at standing nose height from the floor.

Teaching *rollover* is best started from the down position, with the dog lying on one side, or at least with both hind legs stretched out on the same side. Say "Fido, bang!" and move the lure backwards and alongside the dog's muzzle to its elbow (on the side of its outstretched hind legs). Once the dog looks to the side and backwards, very slowly move the lure upwards to the dog's shoulder and backbone. Tickling the dog in the goolies (groin area) often invokes a reflex-raising of the hind leg as an appeasement gesture, which facilitates the tendency to roll over. If you move the lure too quickly and the dog jumps into the standing position, have patience and start again. As soon as the dog rolls onto its back, keep the lure stationary and mesmerize the dog with a relaxing tummy rub.

To teach *rollover-stay* when the dog is standing or moving, say "Fido, bang!" and give the appropriate hand signal (with index finger pointed and thumb cocked in true Sam Spade fashion), then in one fluid movement lure him to first lie down and then rollover-stay as above.

Teaching the dog to *stay* in each of the above four positions becomes a piece of cake after first teaching the dog not to worry at the toy or treat training lure. This is best accomplished by hand feeding dinner kibble. Hold a piece of kibble firmly in your hand and softly instruct "Off!" Ignore any licking and slobbering *for however long the dog worries at the treat,* but say "Take it!" and offer the kibble *the instant* the dog breaks contact with his muzzle. Repeat this a few times, and then up the ante and insist the dog remove his muzzle for one whole second before offering the kibble. Then progressively refine your criteria and have the dog not touch your hand (or treat) for longer and longer periods on each trial, such as for two seconds, four seconds, then six, ten, fifteen, twenty, thirty seconds and so on. The dog soon learns: (1) worrying at the treat never gets results, whereas (2) noncontact is often rewarded after a variable time lapse.

Teaching "*Off!*" has many useful applications in its own right. Additionally, instructing the dog not to touch a training lure often produces spontaneous and magical stays. Request the dog to stand-stay, for example, and not to touch the lure. At first set your sights on a short two-second stay before rewarding the dog. (Remember, every long journey begins with a single step.) However, on subsequent trials, gradually and progressively increase the length of stay required to receive a reward. In no time at all your dog will stand calmly for a minute or so.

Relevancy Training

Once you have taught the dog what you expect her to do when requested to come, sit, lie down, stand, rollover and stay, the time is right to teach the dog *why* she should comply with your wishes. The secret is to have many (*many*) extremely short training interludes (two to five seconds each) at numerous (*numerous*) times during the course of the dog's day. Especially work with the dog immediately *before* the dog's good times and *during* the dog's good times. For example, ask your dog to sit and/or lie down each time before opening doors, serving meals, offering treats and tummy rubs; ask the dog to perform a few controlled doggy push-ups before letting her off-leash or throwing a tennis ball; and perhaps request the dog to sit-down-sit-stand-down-stand-rollover before inviting her to cuddle on the couch.

Similarly, request the dog to sit many times during play or on walks, and in no time at all the dog will be only too pleased to follow your instructions because he has learned that a compliant response heralds all sorts of goodies. Basically all you are trying to teach the dog is how to say please: "Please throw the tennis ball. Please may I snuggle on the couch."

Remember, whereas it is important to keep training interludes short, it is equally important to have many short sessions each and every day. The shortest (and most useful) session comprises asking the dog to sit and then go play during a play session. When trained this way, your dog will soon associate training with good times. In fact, the dog may be unable to distinguish between training and good times and, indeed, there should be no distinction. The warped concept that training involves forcing the dog to comply and/or dominating his will is totally at odds with the picture of a truly well-trained dog. In reality, enjoying a game of training with a dog is no different from enjoying a game of backgammon or tennis with a friend; and walking with a dog should be no different from strolling with buddies on the golf course.

Walk by Your Side

Many people attempt to teach a dog to heel by putting him on a leash and physically correcting the dog when he makes mistakes. There are a number of things seriously wrong with this approach, the first being that most people do not want precision heeling; rather, they simply want the dog to follow or walk by their side. Second, when physically restrained during "training," even though the dog may grudgingly mope by your side when "handcuffed" on leash, let's see what happens when he is off leash. History! The dog is in the next county because he never enjoyed walking with you on leash and you have no control over him off leash. So let's just teach the dog off leash from the outset to *want* to walk with us. Third, if the dog has not been trained to heel, it is a trifle hasty to think about punishing the poor dog for making mistakes and breaking heeling rules he didn't even know existed. This is simply not fair! Surely, if the dog had been adequately taught how to heel, he would seldom make mistakes and hence there would be no need to correct the dog. Remember, each mistake and each correction (punishment) advertise the trainer's inadequacy, not the dog's. The dog is not stubborn, he is not stupid and he is not bad. Even if he were, he would still require training, so let's train him properly.

Let's teach the dog to *enjoy* following us and to *want* to walk by our side offleash. Then it will be easier to teach high-precision off-leash heeling patterns if desired. After attaching the leash for safety on outdoor walks, but before going anywhere, it is necessary to teach the dog specifically not to pull. Now it will be much easier to teach on-leash walking and heeling because the dog already wants to walk with you, he is familiar with the desired walking and heeling positions and he knows not to pull.

FOLLOWING

Start by training your dog to follow you. Many puppies will follow if you simply walk away from them and maybe click your fingers or chuckle. Adult dogs may require additional enticement to stimulate them to follow, such as a training lure or, at the very least, a lively trainer. To teach the dog to follow: (1) keep walking and (2) walk away from the dog. If the dog attempts to lead or lag, change pace; slow down if the dog forges too far ahead, but speed up if he lags too far behind. Say "Steady!" or "Easy!" each time before you slow down and "Quickly!" or "Hustle!" each time before you speed up, and the dog will learn to change pace on cue. If the dog lags or leads too far, or if he wanders right or left, simply walk quickly in the opposite direction and maybe even run away from the dog and hide.

Practicing is a lot of fun; you can set up a course in your home, yard or park to do this. Indoors, entice the dog to follow upstairs, into a bedroom, into the bathroom, downstairs, around the living room couch, zigzagging between dining room chairs and into the kitchen for dinner. Outdoors, get the dog to follow around park benches, trees, shrubs and along walkways and lines in the grass. (For safety outdoors, it is advisable to attach a long line on the dog, but never exert corrective tension on the line.)

Remember, following has a lot to do with attitude—
your attitude! Most probably your dog will *not* want to
follow Mr. Grumpy Troll with the personality of wilted
lettuce. Lighten up—walk with a jaunty step, whistle a
happy tune, sing, skip and tell jokes to your dog and he
will be right there by your side.

BY YOUR SIDE

It is smart to train the dog to walk close on one side or
the other—either side will do, your choice. When walking, jogging or cycling, it is generally bad news to have
the dog suddenly cut in front of you. In fact, I train my
dogs to walk "By my side" and "Other side"—both very
useful instructions. It is possible to position the dog
fairly accurately by looking to the appropriate side and
clicking your fingers or slapping your thigh on that
side. A precise positioning may be attained by holding
a training lure, such as a chewtoy, tennis ball, or food
treat. Stop and stand still several times throughout the
walk, just as you would when window shopping or
meeting a friend. Use the lure to make sure the dog
slows down and stays close whenever you stop.

When teaching the dog to heel, we generally want
her to sit in heel position when we stop. Teach heel

*Using a toy to teach sit-heel-sit sequences: 1) "Phoenix, heel!" Standing still, move lure up and back
over dog's muzzle.... 2) To position dog sitting in heel position on your left side. 3) "Phoenix, heel!"
wagging lure in left hand. Change lure to right hand in preparation for sit signal.*

122

position at the standstill and the dog will learn that the default heel position is sitting by your side (left or right—your choice, unless you wish to compete in obedience trials, in which case the dog must heel on the left).

Several times a day, stand up and call your dog to come and sit in heel position—"Fido, heel!" For example, instruct the dog to come to heel each time there are commercials on TV, or each time you turn a page of a novel, and the dog will get it in a single evening.

Practice straight-line heeling and turns separately. With the dog sitting at heel, teach him to turn in place. After each quarter-turn, half-turn or full turn in place, lure the dog to sit at heel. Now it's time for short straight-line heeling sequences, no more than a few steps at a time. Always think of heeling in terms of Sit-Heel-Sit sequences—start and end with the dog in position and do your best to keep him there when moving. Progressively increase the number of steps in each sequence. When the dog remains close for 20 yards of straight-line heeling, it is time to add a few turns and then sign up for a happy-heeling obedience class to get some advice from the experts.

4) Use hand signal only to lure dog to sit as you stop. Eventually, dog will sit automatically at heel whenever you stop. 5) "Good dog!"

No Pulling on Leash

You can start teaching your dog not to pull on leash anywhere—in front of the television or outdoors—but regardless of location, you must not take a single step with tension in the leash. For a reason known only to dogs, even just a couple of paces of pulling on leash is intrinsically motivating and diabolically rewarding. Instead, attach the leash to the dog's collar, grasp the other end firmly with both hands held close to your chest, and stand still—do not budge an inch. Have somebody watch you with a stopwatch to time your progress, or else you will never believe this will work and so you will not even try the exercise, and your shoulder and the dog's neck will be traumatized for years to come.

Stand still and wait for the dog to stop pulling, and to sit and/or lie down. All dogs stop pulling and sit eventually. Most take only a couple of minutes; the all-time record is 22 ⅕ minutes. Time how long it takes. Gently praise the dog when he stops pulling, and as soon as he sits, enthusiastically praise the dog and take just one step forwards, then immediately stand still. This single step usually demonstrates the ballistic reinforcing nature of pulling on leash; most dogs explode to the end of the leash, so be prepared for the strain. Stand firm and wait for the dog to sit again. Repeat this half a dozen times and you will probably notice a progressive reduction in the force of the dog's one-step explosions and a radical reduction in the time it takes for the dog to sit each time.

As the dog learns "Sit we go" and "Pull we stop," she will begin to walk forward calmly with each single step and automatically sit when you stop. Now try two steps before you stop. Wooooooo! Scary! When the dog has mastered two steps at a time, try for three. After each success, progressively increase the number of steps in the sequence: try four steps and then six, eight, ten and twenty steps before stopping. Congratulations! You are now walking the dog on leash.

Whenever walking with the dog (off leash or on leash), make sure you stop periodically to practice a few position commands and stays before instructing the dog to "Walk on!" (Remember, you want the dog to be compliant everywhere, not just in the kitchen when his dinner is at hand.) For example, stopping every 25 yards to briefly train the dog amounts to over 200 training interludes within a single three-mile stroll. And each training session is in a different location. You will not believe the improvement within just the first mile of the first walk.

To put it another way, integrating training into a walk offers 200 separate opportunities to use the continuance of the walk as a reward to reinforce the dog's education. Moreover, some training interludes may comprise continuing education for the dog's walking skills: Alternate short periods of the dog walking calmly by your side with periods when the dog is allowed to sniff and investigate the environment. Now sniffing odors on the grass and meeting other dogs become rewards which reinforce the dog's calm and mannerly demeanor. Good Lord! Whatever next? Many enjoyable walks together of course. Happy trails!

THE IMPORTANCE OF TRICKS

Nothing will improve a dog's quality of life better than having a few tricks under its belt. Teaching any trick expands the dog's vocabulary, which facilitates communication and improves the owner's control. Also, specific tricks help prevent and resolve specific behavior problems. For example, by teaching the dog to fetch his toys, the dog learns carrying a toy makes the owner happy and, therefore, will be more likely to chew his toy than other inappropriate items.

More important, teaching tricks prompts owners to lighten up and train with a sunny disposition. Really, tricks should be no different from any other behaviors we put on cue. But they are. When teaching tricks, owners have a much sweeter attitude, which in turn motivates the dog and improves her willingness to comply. The dog feels tricks are a blast, but formal commands are a drag. In fact, tricks are so enjoyable, they may be used as rewards in training by asking the dog to come, sit and down-stay and then rollover for a tummy rub. Go on, try it: Crack a smile and even giggle when the dog promptly and willingly lies down and stays.

Most important, performing tricks prompts onlookers to smile and giggle. Many people are scared of dogs, especially large ones. And nothing can be more off-putting for a dog than to be constantly confronted by strangers who don't like him because of his size or the way he looks. Uneasy people put the dog on edge, causing him to back off and bark, only frightening people all the more. And so a vicious circle develops, with the people's fear fueling the dog's fear *and vice versa.* Instead, tie a pink ribbon to your dog's collar and practice all sorts of tricks on walks and in the park, and you will be pleasantly amazed how it changes people's attitudes toward your friendly dog. The dog's repertoire of tricks is limited only by the trainer's imagination. Below I have described three of my favorites:

SPEAK AND SHUSH

The training sequence involved in teaching a dog to bark on request is no different from that used when training any behavior on cue: request—lure—response—reward. As always, the secret of success lies in finding an effective lure. If the dog always barks at the doorbell, for example, say "Rover, speak!", have an accomplice ring the doorbell, then reward the dog for barking. After a few woofs, ask Rover to "Shush!", waggle a food treat under his nose (to entice him to sniff and thus to shush), praise him when quiet and eventually offer the treat as a reward. Alternate "Speak" and "Shush," progressively increasing the length of shush-time between each barking bout.

PLAYBOW

With the dog standing, say "Bow!" and lower the food lure (palm upwards) to rest between the dog's forepaws. Praise as the dog lowers

her forequarters and sternum to the ground (as when teaching the down), but then lure the dog to stand and offer the treat. On successive trials, gradually increase the length of time the dog is required to remain in the playbow posture in order to gain a food reward. If the dog's rear end collapses into a down, say nothing and offer no reward; simply start over.

BE A BEAR

With the dog sitting backed into a corner to prevent him from toppling over backwards, say "Be a Bear!" With bent paw and palm down, raise a lure upwards and backwards along the top of the dog's muzzle. Praise the dog when he sits up on his haunches and offer the treat as a reward. To prevent the dog from standing on his hind legs, keep the lure closer to the dog's muzzle. On each trial, progressively increase the length of time the dog is required to sit up to receive a food reward. Since lure/ reward training is so easy, teach the dog to stand and walk on his hind legs as well!

Teaching "Be a Bear"

chapter 9

Getting
Active
with your Dog

by Bardi McLennan

Once you and your dog have graduated from basic obedience training and are beginning to work together as a team, you can take part in the growing world of dog activities. There are so many fun things to do with your dog! Just remember, people and dogs don't always learn at the same pace, so don't be upset if you (or your dog) need more than two basic training courses before your team becomes operational. Even smart dogs don't go straight to college from kindergarten!

Just as there are events geared to certain types of dogs, so there are ones that are more appealing to certain types of people. In some activities, you give the commands and your dog does the work (upland game hunting is one example), while in others, such as agility, you'll both get a workout. You may want to aim for prestigious titles to add to your dog's name, or you may want nothing more than the sheer enjoyment of being around other people and their dogs. Passive or active, participation has its own rewards.

Consider your dog's physical capabilities when looking into any of the canine activities. It's easy to see that a Basset Hound is not built for the racetrack, nor would a Chihuahua be the breed of choice for pulling a sled. A loyal dog will attempt almost anything you ask him to do, so it is up to you to know your dog's limitations. A dog must be physically sound in order to compete at any level in athletic activities, and being mentally sound is a definite plus. Advanced age, however, may not be a deterrent. Many dogs still hunt and herd at ten or twelve years of age. It's entirely possible for dogs to be "fit at 50." Take your dog for a checkup, explain to your vet the type of activity you have in mind and be guided by his or her findings.

All dogs seem to love playing flyball.

You needn't be restricted to breed-specific sports if it's only fun you're after. Certain AKC activities are limited to designated breeds; however, as each new trial, test or sport has grown in popularity, so has the variety of breeds encouraged to participate at a fun level.

But don't shortchange your fun, or that of your dog, by thinking only of the basic function of her breed. Once a dog has learned how to learn, she can be taught to do just about anything as long as the size of the dog is right for the job and you both think it is fun and rewarding. In other words, you are a team.

To get involved in any of the activities detailed in this chapter, look for the names and addresses of the organizations that sponsor them in Chapter 13. You can also ask your breeder or a local dog trainer for contacts.

You can compete in obedience trials with a well trained dog.

Official American Kennel Club Activities

The following tests and trials are some of the events sanctioned by the AKC and sponsored by various dog clubs. Your dog's expertise will be rewarded with impressive titles. You can participate just for fun, or be competitive and go for those awards.

OBEDIENCE

Training classes begin with pups as young as three months of age in kindergarten puppy training, then advance to pre-novice (all exercises on lead) and go on to novice, which is where you'll start off-lead work. In obedience classes dogs learn to sit, stay, heel and come through a variety of exercises. Once you've got the basics down, you can enter obedience trials and work toward earning your dog's first degree, a C.D. (Companion Dog).

The next level is called "Open," in which jumps and retrieves perk up the dog's interest. Passing grades in competition at this level earn a C.D.X. (Companion Dog Excellent). Beyond that lies the goal of the most ambitious—Utility (U.D. and even U.D.X. or OTCh, an Obedience Champion).

AGILITY

All dogs can participate in the latest canine sport to have gained worldwide popularity for its fun and excitement, agility. It began in England as a canine version of horse show-jumping, but because dogs are more agile and able to perform on verbal commands, extra feats were added such as climbing, balancing and racing through tunnels or in and out of weave poles. Many of the obstacles (regulation or homemade) can be set up in your own backyard. If the agility bug bites, you could end up in international competition!

For starters, your dog should be obedience trained, even though, in the beginning, the lessons may all be taught on lead. Once the dog understands the commands (and you do, too), it's as easy as guiding the dog over a prescribed course, one obstacle at a time. In competition, the race is against the clock, so wear your running shoes! The dog starts with 200 points and the judge deducts for infractions and misadventures along the way.

All dogs seem to love agility and respond to it as if they were being turned loose in a playground paradise. Your dog's enthusiasm will be contagious; agility turns into great fun for dog and owner.

FIELD TRIALS AND HUNTING TESTS

There are field trials and hunting tests for the sporting breeds—retrievers, spaniels and pointing breeds, and for some hounds—Bassets, Beagles and Dachshunds. Field trials are competitive events that test a dog's ability to perform the functions for which she was bred. Hunting tests, which are open to retrievers,

---

TITLES AWARDED BY THE AKC

Conformation: Ch. (Champion)

Obedience: CD (Companion Dog); CDX (Companion Dog Excellent); UD (Utility Dog); UDX (Utility Dog Excellent); OTCh. (Obedience Trial Champion)

Field: JH (Junior Hunter); SH (Senior Hunter); MH (Master Hunter); AFCh. (Amateur Field Champion); FCh. (Field Champion)

Lure Coursing: JC (Junior Courser); SC (Senior Courser)

Herding: HT (Herding Tested); PT (Pre-Trial Tested); HS (Herding Started); HI (Herding Intermediate); HX (Herding Excellent); HCh. (Herding Champion)

Tracking: TD (Tracking Dog); TDX (Tracking Dog Excellent)

Agility: NAD (Novice Agility); OAD (Open Agility); ADX (Agility Excellent); MAX (Master Agility)

Earthdog Tests: JE (Junior Earthdog); SE (Senior Earthdog); ME (Master Earthdog)

Canine Good Citizen: CGC

Combination: DC (Dual Champion—Ch. and Fch.); TC (Triple Champion—Ch., Fch., and OTCh.)

---

spaniels and pointing breeds only, are noncompetitive and are a means of judging the dog's ability as well as that of the handler.

Hunting is a very large and complex part of canine sports, and if you own one of the breeds that hunts, the events are a great treat for your dog and you. He gets to do what he was bred for, and you get to work with him and watch him do it. You'll be proud of and amazed at what your dog can do.

Fortunately, the AKC publishes a series of booklets on these events, which outline the rules and regulations and include a glossary of the sometimes complicated terms. The AKC also publishes newsletters for field trialers and hunting test enthusiasts. The United Kennel Club (UKC) also has informative materials for the hunter and his dog.

Retrievers and other sporting breeds get to do what they're bred to in hunting tests.

HERDING TESTS AND TRIALS

Herding, like hunting, dates back to the first known uses man made of dogs. The interest in herding today is widespread, and if you own a herding breed, you can join in the activity. Herding dogs are tested for their natural skills to keep a flock of ducks, sheep or cattle together. If your dog shows potential, you can start at the testing level, where your dog can earn a title for showing an inherent herding ability. With training you can advance to the trial level, where your dog should be capable of controlling even difficult livestock in diverse situations.

LURE COURSING

The AKC Tests and Trials for Lure Coursing are open to traditional sighthounds—Greyhounds, Whippets,

Borzoi, Salukis, Afghan Hounds, Ibizan Hounds and Scottish Deerhounds—as well as to Basenjis and Rhodesian Ridgebacks. Hounds are judged on overall ability, follow, speed, agility and endurance. This is possibly the most exciting of the trials for spectators, because the speed and agility of the dogs is awesome to watch as they chase the lure (or "course") in heats of two or three dogs at a time.

TRACKING

This tracking dog is hot on the trail.

Tracking is another activity in which almost any dog can compete because every dog that sniffs the ground when taken outdoors is, in fact, tracking. The hard part comes when the rules as to what, when and where the dog tracks are determined by a person, not the dog! Tracking tests cover a large area of fields, woods and roads. The tracks are laid hours before the dogs go to work on them, and include "tricks" like cross-tracks and sharp turns. If you're interested in search-and-rescue work, this is the place to start.

EARTHDOG TESTS FOR SMALL TERRIERS AND DACHSHUNDS

These tests are open to Australian, Bedlington, Border, Cairn, Dandie Dinmont, Smooth and Wire Fox, Lakeland, Norfolk, Norwich, Scottish, Sealyham, Skye, Welsh and West Highland White Terriers as well as Dachshunds. The dogs need no prior training for this terrier sport. There is a qualifying test on the day of the event, so dog and handler learn the rules on the spot. These tests, or "digs," sometimes end with informal races in the late afternoon.

Here are some of the extracurricular obedience and racing activities that are not regulated by the AKC or UKC, but are generally run by clubs or a group of dog fanciers and are often open to all.

Canine Freestyle This activity is something new on the scene and is variously likened to dancing, dressage or ice skating. It is meant to show the athleticism of the dog, but also requires showmanship on the part of the dog's handler. If you and your dog like to ham it up for friends, you might want to look into freestyle.

Lure coursing lets sighthounds do what they do best—run!

Scent Hurdle Racing Scent hurdle racing is purely a fun activity sponsored by obedience clubs with members forming competing teams. The height of the hurdles is based on the size of the shortest dog on the team. On a signal, one team dog is released on each of two side-by-side courses and must clear every hurdle before picking up its own dumbbell from a platform and returning over the jumps to the handler. As each dog returns, the next on that team is sent. Of course, that is what the dogs are supposed to do. When the dogs improvise (going under or around the hurdles, stealing another dog's dumbbell, and so forth), it no doubt frustrates the handlers, but just adds to the fun for everyone else.

Flyball This type of racing is similar, but after negotiating the four hurdles, the dog comes to a flyball box, steps on a lever that releases a tennis ball into the air, catches the ball and returns over the hurdles to the starting point. This game also becomes extremely fun for spectators because the dogs sometimes cheat by catching a ball released by the dog in the next lane. Three titles can be earned—Flyball Dog (F.D.), Flyball Dog Excellent (F.D.X.) and Flyball Dog Champion (Fb.D.Ch.)—all awarded by the North American Flyball Association, Inc.

Dogsledding The name conjures up the Rocky Mountains or the frigid North, but you can find dogsled clubs in such unlikely spots as Maryland, North Carolina and Virginia! Dogsledding is primarily for the Nordic breeds such as the Alaskan Malamutes, Siberian Huskies and Samoyeds, but other breeds can try. There are some practical backyard applications to this sport, too. With parental supervision, almost any strong dog could pull a child's sled.

Coming over the A-frame on an agility course.

These are just some of the many recreational ways you can get to know and understand your multifaceted dog better and have fun doing it.

chapter 10

Your Dog
and your
Family

by Bardi McLennan

Adding a dog automatically increases your family by one, no matter whether you live alone in an apartment or are part of a mother, father and six kids household. The single-person family is fair game for numerous and varied canine misconceptions as to who is dog and who pays the bills, whereas a dog in a houseful of children will consider himself to be just one of the gang, littermates all. One dog and one child may give a dog reason to believe they are both kids or both dogs. Either interpretation requires parental supervision and sometimes speedy intervention.

As soon as one paw goes through the door into your home, Rufus (or Rufina) has to make many adjustments to become a part of your family. Your job is to make him fit in as painlessly as possible. An older dog may have some frame of reference from past experience, but to a 10-week-old puppy, everything is brand new: people, furniture, stairs, when and where people eat, sleep or watch TV, his own place and everyone else's space, smells, sounds, outdoors—everything!

Puppies, and newly acquired dogs of any age, do not need what we think of as "freedom." If you leave a new dog or puppy loose in the house, you will almost certainly return to chaotic destruction and the dog will forever after equate your homecoming with a time of punishment to be dreaded. It is unfair to give your dog what amounts to "freedom to get into trouble." Instead, confine him to a crate for brief periods of your absence (up to three or four hours) and, for the long haul, a workday for example, confine him to one untrashable area with his own toys, a bowl of water and a radio left on (low) in another room.

Lots of pets get along with each other just fine.

For the first few days, when not confined, put Rufus on a long leash tied to your wrist or waist. This umbilical cord method enables the dog to learn all about you from your body language and voice, and to learn by his own actions which things in the house are NO! and which ones are rewarded by "Good dog." Housetraining will be easier with the pup always by your side. Speaking of which, accidents do happen. That goal of "completely housetrained" takes up to a year, or the length of time it takes the pup to mature.

The All-Adult Family

Most dogs in an adults-only household today are likely to be latchkey pets, with no one home all day but the dog. When you return after a tough day on the job, the dog can and should be your relaxation therapy. But going home can instead be a daily frustration.

Separation anxiety is a very common problem for the dog in a working household. It may begin with whines and barks of loneliness, but it will soon escalate into a frenzied destruction derby. That is why it is so important to set aside the time to teach a dog to relax when left alone in his confined area and to understand that he can trust you to return.

Let the dog get used to your work schedule in easy stages. Confine him to one room and go in and out of that room over and over again. Be casual about it. No physical, voice or eye contact. When the pup no longer even notices your comings and goings, leave the house for varying lengths of time, returning to stay home for a few minutes and gradually increasing the time away. This training can take days, but the dog is learning that you haven't left him forever and that he can trust you.

Any time you leave the dog, but especially during this training period, be casual about your departure. No anxiety-building fond farewells. Just "Bye" and go! Remember the "Good dog" when you return to find everything more or less as you left it.

If things are a mess (or even a disaster) when you return, greet the dog, take him outside to eliminate, and then put him in his crate while you clean up. Rant and rave in the shower! *Do not* punish the dog. You were not there when it happened, and the rule is: Only punish as you catch the dog in the act of wrongdoing. Obviously, it makes sense to get your latchkey puppy when you'll have a week or two to spend on these training essentials.

Family weekend activities should include Rufus whenever possible. Depending on the pup's age, now is the time for a long walk in the park, playtime in the backyard, a hike in the woods. Socializing is as important as health care, good food and physical exercise, so visiting Aunt Emma or Uncle Harry and the next-door neighbor's dog or cat is essential to developing an outgoing, friendly temperament in your pet.

If you are a single adult, socializing Rufus at home and away will prevent him from becoming overly protective of you (or just overly attached) and will also prevent such behavioral problems as dominance or fear of strangers.

Babies

Whether already here or on the way, babies figure larger than life in the eyes of a dog. If the dog is there first, let him in on all your baby preparations in the house. When baby arrives, let Rufus sniff any item of clothing that has been on the baby before Junior comes home. Then let Mom greet the dog first before introducing the new family member. Hold the baby down for the dog to see and sniff, but make sure someone's holding the dog on lead in case of any sudden moves. Don't play keep-away or tease the dog with the baby, which only invites undesirable jumping up.

The dog and the baby are "family," and for starters can be treated almost as equals. Things rapidly change, however, especially when baby takes to creeping around on all fours on the dog's turf or, better yet, has yummy pudding all over her face and hands! That's when a lot of things in the dog's and baby's lives become more separate than equal.

Dogs are perfect confidants.

Toddlers make terrible dog owners, but if you can't avoid the combination, use patient discipline (that is, positive teaching rather than punishment), and use time-outs before you run out of patience.

A dog and a baby (or toddler, or an assertive young child) should never be left alone together. Take the dog with you or confine him. With a baby or youngsters in the house, you'll have plenty of use for that wonderful canine safety device called a crate!

Young Children

Any dog in a house with kids will behave pretty much as the kids do, good or bad. But even good dogs and good children can get into trouble when play becomes rowdy and active.

Teach children how to play nicely with a puppy.

Legs bobbing up and down, shrill voices screeching, a ball hurtling overhead, all add up to exuberant frustration for a dog who's just trying to be part of the gang. In a pack of puppies, any legs or toys being chased would be caught by a set of teeth, and all the pups involved would understand that is how the game is played. Kids do not understand this, nor do parents tolerate it. Bring Rufus indoors before you have reason to regret it. This is time-out, not a punishment.

You can explain the situation to the children and tell them they must play quieter games until the puppy learns not to grab them with his mouth. Unfortunately, you can't explain it that easily to the dog. With adult supervision, they will learn how to play together.

Young children love to tease. Sticking their faces or wiggling their hands or fingers in the dog's face is teasing. To another person it might be just annoying, but it is threatening to a dog. There's another difference: We can make the child stop by an explanation, but the only way a dog can stop it is with a warning growl and then with teeth. Teasing is the major cause of children being bitten by their pets. Treat it seriously.

Older Children

The best age for a child to get a first dog is between the ages of 8 and 12. That's when kids are able to accept some real responsibility for their pet. Even so, take the child's vow of "I will never *ever* forget to feed (brush, walk, etc.) the dog" for what it's worth: a child's good intention at that moment. Most kids today have extra lessons, soccer practice, Little League, ballet, and so forth piled on top of school schedules. There will be many times when Mom will have to come to the dog's rescue. "I walked the dog for you so you can set the table for me" is one way to get around a missed appointment without laying on blame or guilt.

Kids in this age group make excellent obedience trainers because they are into the teaching/learning process themselves and they lack the self-consciousness of adults. Attending a dog show is something the whole family can enjoy, and watching Junior Showmanship may catch the eye of the kids. Older children can begin to get involved in many of the recreational activities that were reviewed in the previous chapter. Some of the agility obstacles, for example, can be set up in the backyard as a family project (with an adult making sure all the equipment is safe and secure for the dog).

Older kids are also beginning to look to the future, and may envision themselves as veterinarians or trainers or show dog handlers or writers of the next Lassie best-seller. Dogs are perfect confidants for these dreams. They won't tell a soul.

Other Pets

Introduce all pets tactfully. In a dog/cat situation, hold the dog, not the cat. Let two dogs meet on neutral turf—a stroll in the park or a walk down the street—with both on loose leads to permit all the normal canine ways of saying hello, including routine sniffing, circling, more sniffing, and so on. Small creatures such as hamsters, chinchillas or mice must be kept safe from their natural predators (dogs and cats).

Festive Family Occasions

Parties are great for people, but not necessarily for puppies. Until all the guests have arrived, put the dog in his crate or in a room where he won't be disturbed. A socialized dog can join the fun later as long as he's not underfoot, annoying guests or into the hors d'oeuvres.

There are a few dangers to consider, too. Doors opening and closing can allow a puppy to slip out unnoticed in the confusion, and you'll be organizing a search party instead of playing host or hostess. Party food and buffet service are not for dogs. Let Rufus party in his crate with a nice big dog biscuit.

At Christmas time, not only are tree decorations dangerous and breakable (and perhaps family heirlooms), but extreme caution should be taken with the lights, cords and outlets for the tree lights and any other festive lighting. Occasionally a dog lifts a leg, ignoring the fact that the tree is indoors. To avoid this, use a canine repellent, made for gardens, on the tree. Or keep him out of the tree room unless supervised. And whatever you do, *don't* invite trouble by hanging his toys on the tree!

Car Travel

Before you plan a vacation by car or RV with Rufus, be sure he enjoys car travel. Nothing spoils a holiday quicker than a carsick dog! Work within the dog's comfort level. Get in the car with the dog in his crate or attached to a canine car safety belt and just sit there until he relaxes. That's all. Next time, get in the car, turn on the engine and go nowhere. Just sit. When that is okay, turn on the engine and go around the block. Now you can go for a ride and include a stop where you get out, leaving the dog for a minute or two.

On a warm day, always park in the shade and leave windows open several inches. And return quickly. It only takes 10 minutes for a car to become an overheated steel death trap.

Motel or Pet Motel?

Not all motels or hotels accept pets, but you have a much better choice today than even a few years ago. To find a dog-friendly lodging, look at *On the Road Again With Man's Best Friend,* a series of directories that detail bed and breakfasts, inns, family resorts and other hotels/motels. Some places require a refundable deposit to cover any damage incurred by the dog. More B&Bs accept pets now, but some restrict the size.

If taking Rufus with you is not feasible, check out boarding kennels in your area. Your veterinarian may offer this service, or recommend a kennel or two he or she is familiar with. Go see the facilities for yourself, ask about exercise, diet, housing, and so on. Or, if you'd rather have Rufus stay home, look into bonded petsitters, many of whom will also bring in the mail and water your plants.

chapter 11

Your Dog
and your
Community

by Bardi McLennan

Step outside your home with your dog and you are no longer just family, you are both part of your community. This is when the phrase "responsible pet ownership" takes on serious implications. For starters, it means you pick up after your dog—not just occasionally, but every time your dog eliminates away from home. That means you have joined the Plastic ᵃggy Brigade! You always have ᵗic sandwich bags in your ᵗ and several in the car. It ᵛou teach your kids how ᵉm, too. If you think ᵧ," just imagine what

ᵃ non-doggy person) who inadvertently steps in the mess

144

Your responsibility extends to your neighbors: To their ears (no annoying barking); to their property (their garbage, their lawn, their flower beds, their cat—especially their cat); to their kids (on bikes, at play); to their kids' toys and sports equipment.

There are numerous dog-related laws, ranging from simple dog licensing and leash laws to those holding you liable for any physical injury or property damage done by your dog. These laws are in place to protect everyone in the community, including you and your dog. There are town ordinances and state laws which are by no means the same in all towns or all states. Ignorance of the law won't get you off the hook. The time to find out what the laws are where you live is now.

Be sure your dog's license is current. This is not just a good local ordinance, it can make the difference between finding your lost dog or not.

Many states now require proof of rabies vaccination and that the dog has been spayed or neutered before issuing a license. At the same time, keep up the dog's annual immunizations.

Dressing your dog up makes him appealing to strangers.

Never let your dog run loose in the neighborhood. This will not only keep you on the right side of the leash law, it's the outdoor version of the rule about not giving your dog "freedom to get into trouble."

Good Canine Citizen

Sometimes it's hard for a dog's owner to assess whether or not the dog is sufficiently socialized to be accepted by the community at large. Does Rufus or Rufina display good, controlled behavior in public? The AKC's Canine Good Citizen program is available through many dog organizations. If your dog passes the test, the title "CGC" is earned.

The overall purpose is to turn your dog into a good neighbor and to teach you about your responsibility to your community as a dog owner. Here are the ten things your dog must do willingly:

1. Accept a stranger stopping to chat with you.
2. Sit and be petted by a stranger.
3. Allow a stranger to handle him or her as a groomer or veterinarian would.
4. Walk nicely on a loose lead.
5. Walk calmly through a crowd.
6. Sit and down on command, then stay in a sit or down position while you walk away.
7. Come when called.
8. Casually greet another dog.
9. React confidently to distractions.
10. Accept being left alone with someone other than you and not become overly agitated or nervous.

Schools and Dogs

Schools are getting involved with pet ownership on an educational level. It has been proven that children who are kind to animals are humane in their attitude toward other people as adults.

A dog is a child's best friend, and so children are often primary pet owners, if not the primary caregivers. Unfortunately, they are also the ones most often bitten by dogs. This occurs due to a lack of understanding that pets, no matter how sweet, cuddly and loving, are still animals. Schools, along with parents, dog clubs, dog fanciers and the AKC, are working to change all that with video programs for children not only in grade school, but in the nursery school and pre-kindergarten age group. Teaching youngsters how to be responsible dog owners is important community work. When your dog has a CGC, volunteer to take part in an educational classroom event put on by your dog club.

Boy Scout Merit Badge

A Merit Badge for Dog Care can be earned by any Boy Scout ages 11 to 18. The requirements are not easy, but amount to a complete course in responsible dog care and general ownership. Here are just a few of the things a Scout must do to earn that badge:

Point out ten parts of the dog using the correct names.

Give a report (signed by parent or guardian) on your care of the dog (feeding, food used, housing, exercising, grooming and bathing), plus what has been done to keep the dog healthy.

Explain the right way to obedience train a dog, and demonstrate three comments.

Several of the requirements have to do with health care, including first aid, handling a hurt dog, and the dangers of home treatment for a serious ailment.

The final requirement is to know the local laws and ordinances involving dogs.

There are similar programs for Girl Scouts and 4-H members.

Local Clubs

Local dog clubs are no longer in existence just to put on a yearly dog show. Today, they are apt to be the hub of the community's involvement with pets. Dog clubs conduct educational forums with big-name speakers, stage demonstrations of canine talent in a busy mall and take dogs of various breeds to schools for classroom discussion.

The quickest way to feel accepted as a member in a club is to volunteer your services! Offer to help with something—anything—and watch your popularity (and your interest) grow.

Therapy Dogs

Once your dog has earned that essential CGC and reliably demonstrates a steady, calm temperament, you could look into what therapy dogs are doing in your area.

Therapy dogs go with their owners to visit patients at hospitals or nursing homes, generally remaining on leash but able to coax a pat from a stiffened hand, a smile from a blank face, a few words from sealed lips or a hug from someone in need of love.

Nursing homes cover a wide range of patient care. Some specialize in care of the elderly, some in the treatment of specific illnesses, some in physical therapy. Children's facilities also welcome visits from trained therapy dogs for boosting morale in their pediatric patients. Hospice care for the terminally ill and the at-home care of AIDS patients are other areas where this canine visiting is desperately needed. Therapy dog training comes first.

Your dog can make a difference in lots of lives.

There is a lot more involved than just taking your nice friendly pooch to someone's bedside. Doing therapy dog work involves your own emotional stability as well as that of your dog. But once you have met all the requirements for this work, making the rounds once a week or once a month with your therapy dog is possibly the most rewarding of all community activities.

Disaster Aid

This community service is definitely not for everyone, partly because it is time-consuming. The initial training is rigorous, and there can be no let-up in the continuing workouts, because members are on call 24 hours a day to go wherever they are needed at a moment's notice. But if you think you would like to be able to assist in a disaster, look into search-and-rescue work. The network of search-and-rescue volunteers is worldwide, and all members of the American Rescue Dog Association (ARDA) who are qualified to do this work are volunteers who train and maintain their own dogs.

Physical Aid

Most people are familiar with Seeing Eye dogs, which serve as blind people's eyes, but not with all the other work that dogs are trained to do to assist the disabled. Dogs are also specially trained to pull wheelchairs, carry school books, pick up dropped objects, open and close doors. Some also are ears for the deaf. All these assistance-trained dogs, by the way, are allowed anywhere "No Pet" signs exist (as are therapy dogs when

properly identified). Getting started in any of this fascinating work requires a background in dog training and canine behavior, but there are also volunteer jobs ranging from answering the phone to cleaning out kennels to providing a foster home for a puppy. You have only to ask.

Making the rounds with your therapy dog can be very rewarding.

part four

Beyond
the
Basics

chapter 12

Recommended Reading

Books

ABOUT HEALTH CARE

Ackerman, Lowell. *Guide to Skin and Haircoat Problems in Dogs*. Loveland, Colo.: Alpine Publications, 1994.

Alderton, David. *The Dog Care Manual*. Hauppauge, N.Y.: Barron's Educational Series, Inc., 1986.

American Kennel Club. *American Kennel Club Dog Care and Training*. New York· Howell Book House, 1991.

Bamberger, Michelle, DVM. *Help! The Quick Guide to First Aid for Your Dog*. New York: Howell Book House, 1995.

Carlson, Delbert, DVM, and James Giffin, MD. *Dog Owner's Home Veterinary Handbook*. New York: Howell Book House, 1992.

DeBitetto, James, DVM, and Sarah Hodgson. *You & Your Puppy*. New York: Howell Book House, 1995.

Humphries, Jim, DVM. *Dr. Jim's Animal Clinic for Dogs*. New York: Howell Book House, 1994.

McGinnis, Terri. *The Well Dog Book*. New York: Random House, 1991.

Pitcairn, Richard and Susan. *Natural Health for Dogs*. Emmaus, Pa.: Rodale Press, 1982.

ABOUT DOG SHOWS

Hall, Lynn. *Dog Showing for Beginners*. New York: Howell Book House, 1994.

Nichols, Virginia Tuck. *How to Show Your Own Dog*. Neptune, N. J.: TFH, 1970.

Vanacore, Connie. *Dog Showing, An Owner's Guide*. New York: Howell Book House, 1990.

ABOUT TRAINING

Ammen, Amy. *Training in No Time.* New York: Howell Book House, 1995.

Baer, Ted. *Communicating With Your Dog.* Hauppauge, N.Y.: Barron's Educational Series, Inc., 1989.

Benjamin, Carol Lea. *Dog Problems.* New York: Howell Book House, 1989.

Benjamin, Carol Lea. *Dog Training for Kids.* New York: Howell Book House, 1988.

Benjamin, Carol Lea. *Mother Knows Best.* New York: Howell Book House, 1985.

Benjamin, Carol Lea. *Surviving Your Dog's Adolescence.* New York: Howell Book House, 1993.

Bohnenkamp, Gwen. *Manners for the Modern Dog.* San Francisco: Perfect Paws, 1990.

Dibra, Bashkim. *Dog Training by Bash.* New York: Dell, 1992.

Dunbar, Ian, PhD, MRCVS. *Dr. Dunbar's Good Little Dog Book,* James & Kenneth Publishers, 2140 Shattuck Ave. #2406, Berkeley, Calif. 94704. (510) 658–8588. Order from the publisher.

Dunbar, Ian, PhD, MRCVS. *How to Teach a New Dog Old Tricks,* James & Kenneth Publishers. Order from the publisher; address above.

Dunbar, Ian, PhD, MRCVS, and Gwen Bohnenkamp. Booklets on *Preventing Aggression; Housetraining; Chewing; Digging; Barking; Socialization; Fearfulness; and Fighting,* James & Kenneth Publishers. Order from the publisher; address above.

Evans, Job Michael. *People, Pooches and Problems.* New York: Howell Book House, 1991.

Kilcommons, Brian and Sarah Wilson. *Good Owners, Great Dogs.* New York: Warner Books, 1992.

McMains, Joel M. *Dog Logic—Companion Obedience.* New York: Howell Book House, 1992.

Rutherford, Clarice and David H. Neil, MRCVS. *How to Raise a Puppy You Can Live With.* Loveland, Colo.: Alpine Publications, 1982.

Volhard, Jack and Melissa Bartlett. *What All Good Dogs Should Know: The Sensible Way to Train.* New York: Howell Book House, 1991.

ABOUT BREEDING

Harris, Beth J. Finder. *Breeding a Litter, The Complete Book of Prenatal and Postnatal Care.* New York: Howell Book House, 1983.

Holst, Phyllis, DVM. *Canine Reproduction.* Loveland, Colo.: Alpine Publications, 1985.

Walkowicz, Chris and Bonnie Wilcox, DVM. *Successful Dog Breeding, The Complete Handbook of Canine Midwifery*. New York: Howell Book House, 1994.

ABOUT ACTIVITIES

American Rescue Dog Association. *Search and Rescue Dogs.* New York: Howell Book House, 1991.

Barwig, Susan and Stewart Hilliard. *Schutzhund.* New York: Howell Book House, 1991.

Beaman, Arthur S. *Lure Coursing.* New York: Howell Book House, 1994.

Daniels, Julie. *Enjoying Dog Agility—From Backyard to Competition.* New York: Doral Publishing, 1990.

Davis, Kathy Diamond. *Therapy Dogs.* New York: Howell Book House, 1992.

Gallup, Davis Anne. *Running With Man's Best Friend.* Loveland, Colo.: Alpine Publications, 1986.

Habgood, Dawn and Robert. *On the Road Again With Man's Best Friend.* New England, Mid-Atlantic, West Coast and Southeast editions. Selective guides to area bed and breakfasts, inns, hotels and resorts that welcome guests and their dogs. New York: Howell Book House, 1995.

Holland, Vergil S. *Herding Dogs.* New York: Howell Book House, 1994.

LaBelle, Charlene G. *Backpacking With Your Dog.* Loveland, Colo.: Alpine Publications, 1993.

Simmons-Moake, Jane. *Agility Training, The Fun Sport for All Dogs.* New York: Howell Book House, 1991.

Spencer, James B. *Hup! Training Flushing Spaniels the American Way.* New York: Howell Book House, 1992.

Spencer, James B. *Point! Training the All-Seasons Birddog.* New York: Howell Book House, 1995.

Tarrant, Bill. *Training the Hunting Retriever.* New York: Howell Book House, 1991.

Volhard, Jack and Wendy. *The Canine Good Citizen.* New York: Howell Book House, 1994.

General Titles

Haggerty, Captain Arthur J. *How to Get Your Pet Into Show Business.* New York: Howell Book House, 1994.

McLennan, Bardi. *Dogs and Kids, Parenting Tips.* New York: Howell Book House, 1993.

Moran, Patti J. *Pet Sitting for Profit, A Complete Manual for Professional Success.* New York: Howell Book House, 1992.

Beyond the
Basics

Scalisi, Danny and Libby Moses. *When Rover Just Won't Do, Over 2,000 Suggestions for Naming Your Dog.* New York: Howell Book House, 1993.

Sife, Wallace, PhD. *The Loss of a Pet.* New York: Howell Book House, 1993.

Wrede, Barbara J. *Civilizing Your Puppy.* Hauppauge, N.Y.: Barron's Educational Series, 1992.

Magazines

The AKC GAZETTE, The Official Journal for the Sport of Purebred Dogs. American Kennel Club, 51 Madison Ave., New York, NY.

Bloodlines Journal. United Kennel Club, 100 E. Kilgore Rd., Kalamazoo, MI.

Dog Fancy. Fancy Publications, 3 Burroughs, Irvine, CA 92718

Dog World. Maclean Hunter Publishing Corp., 29 N. Wacker Dr., Chicago, IL 60606.

Videos

"SIRIUS Puppy Training," by Ian Dunbar, PhD, MRCVS. James & Kenneth Publishers, 2140 Shattuck Ave. #2406, Berkeley, CA 94704. Order from the publisher.

"Training the Companion Dog," from Dr. Dunbar's British TV Series, James & Kenneth Publishers. (See address above).

The American Kennel Club produces videos on every breed of dog, as well as on hunting tests, field trials and other areas of interest to purebred dog owners. For more information, write to AKC/Video Fulfillment, 5580 Centerview Dr., Suite 200, Raleigh, NC 27606.

chapter 13

Resources

Breed Clubs

Every breed recognized by the American Kennel Club has a national (parent) club. National clubs are a great source of information on your breed. You can get the name of the secretary of the club by contacting:

The American Kennel Club
51 Madison Avenue
New York, NY 10010
(212) 696-8200

There are also numerous all-breed, individual breed, obedience, hunting and other special-interest dog clubs across the country. The American Kennel Club can provide you with a geographical list of clubs to find ones in your area. Contact them at the above address.

Registry Organizations

Registry organizations register purebred dogs. The American Kennel Club is the oldest and largest in this country, and currently recognizes over 130 breeds. The United Kennel Club registers some breeds the AKC doesn't (including the American Pit Bull Terrier and the Miniature Fox Terrier) as well as many of the same breeds. The others included here are for your reference; the AKC can provide you with a list of foreign registries.

American Kennel Club
51 Madison Avenue
New York, NY 10010

United Kennel Club (UKC)
100 E. Kilgore Road
Kalamazoo, MI 49001-5598

American Dog Breeders Assn.
P.O. Box 1771
Salt Lake City, UT 84110
(Registers American Pit Bull Terriers)

Canadian Kennel Club
89 Skyway Avenue
Etobicoke, Ontario
Canada M9W 6R4

National Stock Dog Registry
P.O. Box 402
Butler, IN 46721
(Registers working stock dogs)

Orthopedic Foundation for Animals (OFA)
2300 E. Nifong Blvd.
Columbia, MO 65201-3856
(Hip registry)

Activity Clubs

Write to these organizations for information on the activities they sponsor.

American Kennel Club
51 Madison Avenue
New York, NY 10010
(Conformation Shows, Obedience Trials, Field Trials and Hunting Tests, Agility, Canine Good

Associations

American Dog Owners Assn.
1654 Columbia Tpk.
Castleton, NY 12033
(Combats anti-dog legislation)

Delta Society
P.O. Box 1080
Renton, WA 98057-1080
(Promotes the human/animal bond through
pet-assisted therapy and other programs)

Dog Writers Assn. of America (DWAA)
Sally Cooper, Secy.
222 Woodchuck Ln.
Harwinton, CT 06791

National Assn. for Search and Rescue (NASAR)
P.O. Box 3709
Fairfax, VA 22038

Therapy Dogs International
6 Hilltop Road
Mendham, NJ 07945

Citizen, Lure Coursing, Herding, Tracking, Earthdog Tests, Coonhunting.)

United Kennel Club
100 E. Kilgore Road
Kalamazoo, MI 49001-5598
(Conformation Shows, Obedience Trials, Agility, Hunting for Various Breeds, Terrier Trials and more.)

North American Flyball Assn.
1342 Jeff St.
Ypsilanti, MI 48198

International Sled Dog Racing Assn.
P.O. Box 446
Norman, ID 83848-0446

North American Working Dog Assn., Inc.
Southeast Kreisgruppe
P.O. Box 833
Brunswick, GA 31521

Trainers

Association of Pet Dog Trainers
P.O. Box 3734
Salinas, CA 93912
(408) 663–9257

American Dog Trainers' Network
161 West 4th St.
New York, NY 10014
(212) 727–7257

National Association of Dog Obedience Instructors
2286 East Steel Rd.
St. Johns, MI 48879